a little something about the author

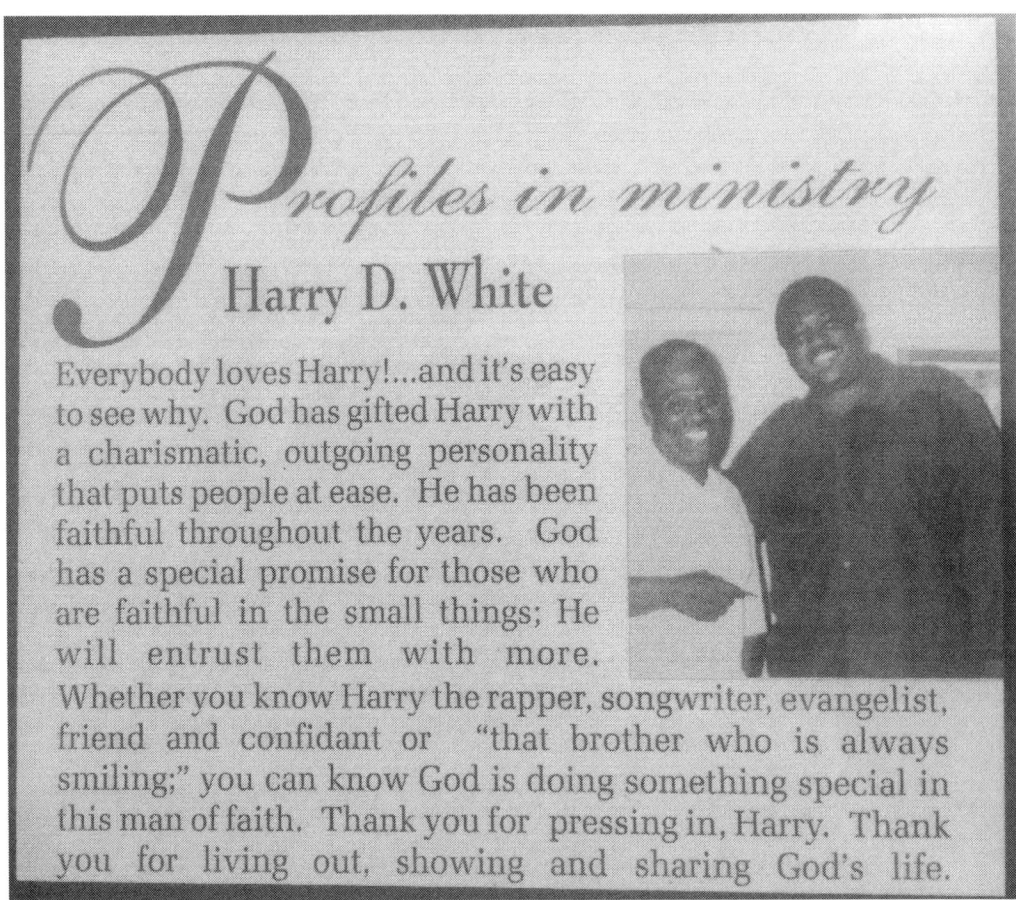

Profiles in ministry

Harry D. White

Everybody loves Harry!...and it's easy to see why. God has gifted Harry with a charismatic, outgoing personality that puts people at ease. He has been faithful throughout the years. God has a special promise for those who are faithful in the small things; He will entrust them with more. Whether you know Harry the rapper, songwriter, evangelist, friend and confidant or "that brother who is always smiling;" you can know God is doing something special in this man of faith. Thank you for pressing in, Harry. Thank you for living out, showing and sharing God's life.

Wanted to show you who helped kick all this off. My street ministry chops came from Liberation Street Church Ministries.

The man in the picture with me is Pastor Charles Moore. A X everything like me who God touched and caused a complete 360degrees turn around. A great mentor whom I'll see on the other side of Jordan in due time.

I also produced a radio show, "Sow Big Radio". I would play the old school gospel songs and speak on them. Pastors would join the show and give a word of knowledge. Some would call in and pray over air.

I had a TV show, can you guess what it's called. "Sow Big TV". I would go into the city and interview people right off the street. Ask them questions about life, about death. What are some of the issues they're going through in this life. It was cool cause when I would turn the camera off they wanted to know more of my view most of the time.

The Light On The Inside Of Us
I'm Gonna Let It Out, What About You?

Why do we live like this? We get pressure from every angle, family, friends, haters, etc. We love The Lord till death simple and plain. That's how deep it's become with us. That's why it is written we are a peculiar people. We practice this love and people are jealous of our zeal for The Lord and they watch us closely for mistakes which I think is a good thing. They won't admittedly say they are, but they will come at you some type of way. Because you love The Lord so much and you speak about Him everyday, people have something against you. They have no idea it's a battle going on inside of themselves. They gonna have to work it out themselves also. God supplied everything they would need to be everything they were called to be. Love'em but can't focus on'em. I focus on The Lord. I do it for The Lord. I do it unto The Lord. I do it before The Lord. It was before The Lord.

    2 Samuel 6:20-21 Then David returned to bless his household. And Michal the daughter of Saul came out to meet David, and said, How glorious was the king of Israel to day, who uncovered himself to day in the eyes of the handmaids of his servants, as one of the vain fellows shamelessly uncovers himself! And David said unto Michal, It was before the Lord, which chose me before thy father, and before all his house, to appoint me ruler over the people of the Lord, over Israel: therefore will I play before the Lord...

    That's what's up! I say to you today that what you get from me is before the Lord who chose me before the foundations of this world! I didn't do it for the slave girls! I didn't do it for the mega church! I didn't do it for the title "007 Da Overseer"! I didn't do it for FB likes or shares! I didn't do it to publish my first book! I did it for The Lord! I do it before the Lord! IT WAS BEFORE THE LORD!!!

    That's how a warrior do. A Life Changer... 007

Foreword

This book is about nuggets. Each page goes deep into this life as we know it and a relationship with the Almighty God. Most of the time it's from a warrior's point of view. Then at times it's from a humbling state cause things went your way better than you could have imagined but not how you planned. God touched your situation and showed Himself strong when you was so week.

It's about praise. How important it is to praise God because He is worthy. The way I praise Him and how some of your testimonies run parallel with mine or not. Just to be able to thank Him, give Him glory is an honor. I speak often in the Spirit cause the Spirit of God is in me. It's just so much, you must read it.

To close out this foreword the best way I can and get my point across would be: Justification, Sanctification, and Glorification. Justification is the action declaring or making righteous in the sight of God. Sanctification is the act of being made holy. Glorification is the action of God's final removal of sin from the life of the believer. I touch on all of this in the way it's been given to me. Hope it's a good read for you.

Oh. One more thing. Before you read, ask God for the Mind of Christ. It will enhance your mind to see more nuggets than you could imagine… 007

TABLE OF CONTENTS

CHRIST WALK REMIX	1
REDZONE	5
WARRIOR	9
SATAN WANT WE TO DIE	14
BALM IN GILEAD	19
AMENNNN	22
TRYIN' TO REACH YA	25
JESUS IS KING	28
TO KNOW ME IS TO KNOW ME	32
WILD HORSES	35
SUCKER FREE	39

SPIRIT STORMIN' IN ME	41
TAKE ON ME	46
CAN YOU HEAR ME NOW	52
YA BLOOD	57
BE NOBODYS FOOL	62
WHERE YA AT?	67
CHOOSE	71
OPPORTUNITY	76
THAT'S CHRISTMAS	79
STRETCH	83
"I'M CRYIN' OUT RIGHT NOW "	87

CHRIST WALK REMIX

Big Up SOC. SOULJAHS of Christ street ministry. San Diego Chapter and all the other chapters in the Body of Christ on the front lines dying to yourselfs, risking your lives that some might be set free. Cause when the Son sets you free, you are free indeed. I'm going in.

HOOK

We walk the streets and we begin to pray. Kinda wish the whole earth would set aside a day. We pray. Wishful thinking. Signs and wonders would follow before you blink and yokes will be broke before weekend, we seeing Christ Walk baby, Christ Walk yea. Christ Walk baby, Christ Walk yea. Christ Walk baby, Christ Walk yea. Christ Walk baby, Christ Walk yea.

1st verse

007 Da Overseer on deck, Jesus Christ mic check, much respect to all da Souljahs, fill ya in later with the rest. Get in where ya fit in. You to near me not to hear me, still let me speak slowly and clearly. I need ya to get this cause it's Kingdom business, somebody been telling you different. God's forgiveness, God's persistence, all my homies ya need to handle ya business. Partake in the Bread of Life, now is the season. This the moment, we have atonement. If y'all ain't on it it's ya own fault. Look again at what you bought, that's the reason ya short. So many benefits come from the King, salvation, a fat calf, a robe, an a ring. Spiritual blessings can't be seen with the naked eye, the gates are open wide. You ain't gotta read between the lines, it's out lined, He's taking all kinds. Cause God is so kind. I asked why, His reply, ALL SOULS ARE MINE. I took out the leaven. ALL SOULS GO TO HEAVEN. Christwalk at 11.

HOOK

We walk the streets and we begin to pray. Kinda wish the whole earth would set aside a day. We pray. Wishful thinking. Signs and wonders would follow before you blink and yokes will be broke before weekend, we seeing Christ Walk baby, Christ Walk yea. Christ Walk baby, Christ

Walk yea. Christ Walk baby, Christ Walk yea. Christ Walk baby, Christ Walk yea.

2nd verse

Imagine Jesus Christ in the streets, and the cops harass Him, bet it happens, was it the captain. I started laughing They harass me to. But I keeps me cool, focus on the task at hand. Having done all to stand. I'm an intricate part of Gods plan, husband, musician, grand pa, business owner, Christian, don't get it twisted. Souljah of Christ to the death in this Christ Walk, it's gonna happen. Valor, Zion, AoG, Wes West, Admin, slapping demons backwards is a daily practice. No actors or actresses. It's on. Jehovah-Jireh, Jehovah-Nissi, Jehovah-Shalom. SK grab da SK, keeps it scripture. Neither SK is carnal, get the picture. Nah mean. See ya on the streets in ya city, any sector, I put that on Souljah Hector. We Believers, Christ Walk all nations. It's HE, not we. Just touching basses.

HOOK

We walk the streets and we begin to pray. Kinda wish the whole earth would set aside a day. We pray. Wishful thinking. Signs and wonders would follow before you blink and yokes will be broke before weekend, we seeing Christ Walk baby, Christ Walk yea. Christ Walk baby, Christ Walk yea. Christ Walk baby, Christ Walk yea. Christ Walk baby, Christ Walk yea.

Mad respect to all believers walking the streets 1,2,3,4 in the morning praying for people. The Kingdom of Heaven is at hand, right in your face in your darkest hour. Big up all street ministries sent by the one true God. Frontlinez Outreach ministry, Durham, I see you. God bless, protect, and add on to us all, in Jesus name

John 21:17
The third time he said to him, "Simon son of John, do you love me?" Peter was hurt because Jesus asked him the third time, "Do you love me?" He said, "Lord,

you know all things; you know that I love you." Jesus said, "**Feed my sheep**.

WHAT INSPIRED ME TO WRITE CHRIST WALK REMIX

I'd have to say it was SOC. Souljah's of Christ. 20 years ago I went to a church called Liberation Street Ministry so I had firsthand experience with the people in the street. You name it, I knew it and whomever. They also knew me. We feed and clothe the poor in our church and went out in the street and met them wherever they were. We would pray for them, take them to appointments. Whatever, we just loved on them or anybody willing to receive our love.

So years later, I ran across a captain in SOC and they showed me much love. They stayed in the street blessing people, praying for people, raising the dead. I fit in like a glove cause we all love the Lord more than a little bit. We love God with madd zeal and it showed.

Now I was in Portland, OR at first so it's a different kind of street than San Diego, CA so you need to have a little knowledge of the street drugs. You could be ministering to someone on weed to someone Chasing the Dragon. Someone might spaz out, pull out a weapon at any given moment. Sometimes knowing the drug can help you react in a certain way to save your live or the person's life.

I don't want to put fear in your heart's, cause you not to go out on Christ Walks but it's trill. You should be trained before you go out on a Christ Walk. You are walking in the natural but acting in the spiritual, the supernatural. Your speaking to the demons in people and on people. You need a gift of decrement out there on the battlefield.

San Diego Christ Walk is different and just as dangerous cause we are at the boarder. So many different languages means more resources, money, gangs, drugs. You're in the middle spreading the goodnews 12am, 1am, 2am in the morning.

People Christ Walk all over America. They believe God for protection. They believe God will save souls from Hell. They believe God will bless them and give them the desires of their hearts. I'm one of them. God gave Captain AOG my name and he gave it to me. I am 007 Da Overseer and I Christ Walk baby, Christ Walk yeah!

REDZONE

1st VERSE

I ain't dead we alive, I'm 50,000 feet in the air and I don't fly. I'm just about to speak in your realm you wanna try. All in good time, this like good times. See it's hard on the Blvd, I bogard the enemy and still get scared. But since Christ be my Lord, I won't be gone till November. It's a year round grind and I'm in my prime. They hit hard but I came with God the Father. 4th quarter redzone sin hitting harder and harder, smarter and smarter, I keeps it official. Take in a deep breath, sin bout to have some issues. I'm backup still in the middle of play, I'm a finish this race at a strong pace, victory I'll taste. Ball back in my hands, this was the plan, for man to stand and have dominion, I do this for my kindren.

2nd VERSE

The flesh must die if I'm a score I gotta get over. I'm no good to you if I don't kill this dude. I'm a Souljah. In an out of my mind, but I was out of my mind, then one day I died. For real, this my testimony on a trac, true story, stretched out, flat on my back. The flesh accomplished that. Then the Lord saw fit to bring me back. Ever since then I been killing the flesh daily. Sometimes it wins, God bless me with a weapon, repentance. Then I win again then I win again flesh recognizes I'm a made man. Can't be snatched out of God's hand. The flesh must die, that's all I'm saying. See somebody went and died for me. Laid down their life that one day my life might be free of sin. There he goes again. And I'm a go again and again telling you about the Son of Man. Yea they hit hard but I came with God the Father. 4th quarter redzone sin hitting harder and harder, smarter and smarter, I keeps it official. Take in a deep breath, sin bout to have some issues. I'm backup still in the middle of play, I'm a finish this race at a strong pace, victory I'll taste. Ball back in my hands, this was the plan, for man to stand and have dominion, I do this for my kindren.

3rd VERSE

Jesus Christ went in, ended all sin, past, present, future. That's gansta, trumps what ya use to. He gave me this gift I gotsta shoot ya. He put aside His crown, came down from deity to humanity. Then into death and hell itself, conquered hell, freed captive souls from satan, so stop hating. Every knee will bow, every toung confess in heaven on earth, under the earth, y'all know the words. They hit hard but I came with God the Father. 4th quarter redzone sin hitting harder and harder, smarter and smarter, I keeps it official. Take in a deep breath, sin bout to have some issues. I'm backup still in the middle of play, I'm a finish this race at a strong pace, victory I'll taste. Ball back in my hands, this was the plan, for man to stand and have dominion, I do this for my kindren.

Talking

They hit hard but I came with God the Father. 4th quarter redzone sin hitting harder and harder, smarter and smarter, I keeps it official. Take in a deep breath, sin bout to have some issues. I'm backup still in the middle of play, I'm a finish this race at a strong pace, victory I'll taste. Ball back in my hands, this was the plan, for man to stand and have dominion, I do this for my kindred

2 Timothy 4:1-7

In the presence of God and of Christ Jesus, who will judge the living and the dead, and in view of his appearing and his kingdom, I give you this charge: 2 Preach the word; be prepared in season and out of season; correct, rebuke and encourage—with great patience and careful instruction. 3 For the time will come when people will not put up with sound doctrine. Instead, to suit their own desires, they will gather around them a great number of teachers to say what their itching ears want to hear. 4 They will turn their ears away from the truth and turn aside to myths. 5 But you,

keep your head in all situations, endure hardship, do the work of an evangelist, discharge all the duties of your ministry.
6 For I am already being poured out like a drink offering, and the time for my departure is near. 7 I have fought the good fight, I have finished the race, I have kept the faith.

WHAT INSPIRED ME TO WRITE REDZONE

I wrote this song not only for me but to encourage the whole Body of Christ. My brothers and my sisters out there on the front lines in the trenches. Just praying for people, loving on people in the name of Jesus. Especially the saints that just became Christian. You're going to war and it's not gonna be easy, but it will be worth it. Time to practice what you believe in. Let it carry over into the game. No question it's on. You're gonna lose friends you thought were your friends. They're gonna talk about you behind your back cause your not with the same ole' same ole' mess. Now you want your moves, your actions to count for something. You wanna score. That's my focus, I gotta score. With Jesus on my side, no weapon formed against me will prosper. I'm gonna be a blessing to this world. Failure is not an option. That's why I gave my life to Jesus Christ.

Not only do you have the ball then but if you drop it, you pick the ball back up and run with it. In other words if you sin, you fall down but get back up. Asked God for forgiveness and get back out there in the fight. Don't be stagnant, no you get back out and fight the good fight of faith because you're going to be a blessing to someone. You're going to be a pillar in the kingdom and that's what this song is about. It's about finishing strong. It's about pressing toward the mark, the high calling God has placed on our lives. I am so preaching to myself right now, thank you Jesus.

Redzone! A warrior song. Describes how I died then was brought back to life in the twinkling of an eye. I wrote about how Jesus laid aside His crown and came down to humanity from deity that we could have a shot at it all. Redzone! How you gonna finish this race. Strong I hope. In the name of Jesus I pray we both score.

WARRIOR

OPEN: Put on the whole armor of God. For we wrestle not against flesh and blood, but against principalities, against powers, against the rulers of the darkness of this world, against spiritual wickedness in high places. Stand firm with the belt of truth, the breastplate of righteousness, your feet fitted with the readiness that comes from the gospel of peace. The shield of faith, The helmet of salvation and the sword of the Spirit, which is the word of God. Pray also for me, that whenever I speak, words may be given me so that I will fearlessly make known the mystery of the gospel. Thank you Lord. Today I become a Warrior.

1verse

I love you Lord now that the world knows it's not hidden, feels like I've been set free broke out of prison. Now amongst the living. Every molecule tripping. Old me very persistent. In a sea of sin I've been forgiven. Now I'm living. The harvest is plentiful, are they gonna listen. The world hates Christians, especially 007, boi I'm on a mission. A fisherman fishing for man I believe I can be affective, the way I used to wreck it all up in the game. I done done some thangs. Now demons know me by name. Things will never be the same. In these war games, Gotta bring da pain. They can't stand the rain. Then there's the thunder, Spiritual Warfare now I'm a wonder. they must run for cover. Find a cave or bunker. I'm more than a conqueror. I can take this land. All in God's plan. Warrior wherever I stand. I declare war. Let the Holy Spirit lead, shall we proceed.

CHORUS

God I'm going all in, you've proved to be more than a friend. A kingdom without end is victorious. Today is the day I become a warrior. Today is the day I become a warrior. A WARRIOR! God I'm going all in, you've proved to be more than a friend. A kingdom without end is victorious. Today is the day I become a warrior. Today is the day I become a warrior. A WARRIOR!

2verse

Thank you for the power, thank you for the peace, thank you for the wisdom, thank you for the grief. West Charlotte, catholic school, San Diego heat. 619, 704, to the 503. Some peep milk some peep meat. I'll preach, I'll teach. Most sleep while I release a force so deep. Welcomed at the dinner table, welcomed in the street. Resurrection power boi the force I speak. In the name of Jesus thank God I see. I'll do you one better you can meet the three. Father, Son, Holy Spirit, they'll make you free. When the Son sets you free you free indeed. I speak to the mountain what you think it will be. I battle the unseen, strongest when I'm weak. He'll raise up a standard, let me follow His lead. This is for the chip, got a 3-0 lead. I'm speaking in the spiritual that's how I be. I wanna put you on while this offer still on the table, this between you and Jesus, He's able, He's the savior.

CHOURS

God I'm going all in, you've proved to be more than a friend. A kingdom without end is victorious. Today is the day I become a warrior. Today is the day I become a warrior. A WARRIOR! God I'm going all in, you've proved to be more than a friend. A kingdom without end is victorious. Today is the day I become a warrior. Today is the day I become a warrior. A WARRIOR!

3verse

This is my story, this is my song an I'm in it to win it. All about the power from His benefits. And this blessing of encouragement, and power stays on my mind from every second to every hour every time. So now I unwind with the Father, dine with the Father. The red carpet treatment for the Father is not a bother. Number one in my life won't have it any other way. You gotta go all in if you want these dividends. You gotta go all in so you can be born again. You gotta go all in Jesus waiting, you can procrastinate if you wanna, the Kingdom of Heaven is a pond ya. Victorious, triumph with the warriors that have answered the call before us. I'm all in, the only way to live. You gotta give till it hurts. To the last becomes first. The first become last. That's how a warrior do, make sure everybody cool.

Everybody good.

CLOSE:

God I'm going all in, you've proved to be more than a friend. A kingdom without end is victorious. Today is the day I become a warrior. Today is the day I become a warrior. A WARRIOR! God I'm going all in, you've proved to be more than a friend. A kingdom without end is victorious. Today is the day I become a warrior. Today is the day I become a warrior. A WARRIOR!

The Armor of God Ephesians 6:10-20

10 Finally, be strong in the Lord and in his mighty power. 11 Put on the full armor of God, so that you can take your stand against the devil's schemes. 12 For our struggle is not against flesh and blood, but against the rulers, against the authorities, against the powers of this dark world and against the spiritual forces of evil in the heavenly realms. 13 Therefore put on the full armor of God, so that when the day of evil comes, you may be able to stand your ground, and after you have done everything, to stand. 14 Stand firm then, with the belt of truth buckled around your waist, with the breastplate of righteousness in place, 15 and with your feet fitted with the readiness that comes from the gospel of peace. 16 In addition to all this, take up the shield of faith, with which you can extinguish all the flaming arrows of the evil one. 17 Take the helmet of salvation and the sword of the Spirit, which is the word of God. 18 And pray in the Spirit on all occasions with all kinds of prayers and requests. With this in mind, be alert and

always keep on praying for all the Lord's people.
19 Pray also for me, that whenever I speak, words may be given me so that I will fearlessly make known the mystery of the gospel, 20 for which I am an ambassador in chains. Pray that I may declare it fearlessly, as I should……

Praise God for all you Warriors in the name of Jesus our Lord and Savior.

WHAT INSPIRED ME TO WRITE WARRIOR

Similar to Redzone as being a battle song but more 411. I'm talking to God but as usual, talking to myself to keep me encouraged. All that God has done for me, don't wanna let Him down. All the 411 He has freely given me, I gotta go to bat for Him. He's proved to be my everything so now I'm going all in. That's what brought on the chorus, "God I'm going all in, you've proved to be more than a friend. A kingdom without end is victorious. Today is the day I become a warrior. Today is the day I become a warrior. A WARRIOR! God I'm going all in, you've proved to be more than a friend. A kingdom without end is victorious. Today is the day I become a warrior. Today is the day I become a warrior. A WARRIOR!"

At the intro, through the body, and at the end incase you've missed it. This is what a Spiritual Warrior would look like.

SATAN WANT WE TO DIE

Open:

You know the commandments: 'You shall not murder, you shall not commit adultery, you shall not steal, you shall not give false testimony, you shall not defraud, honor your father and mother.'" Nobody wanna hear this nowadays. Check it. Nobody's perfect. You need to try. Practice these actions. We are God's people and the first sight of sin should grieve our soul. Yea I'm upset cause I want the best for every human breathing. That's my heart y'all.

1 VERSE:

This is no dream, even though I seem to be extreme, seeing the unseen, in JC I do all things. Don't try to calm me, I won't take no falls. Bawls outside of music hall close calls. Just Satan with his usual rag dolls, obscene calls. Jealous cause of applause and yes yes y'alls. Paul's purpose is my purpose also, to bring as many souls to the savior that wanna go. I don't pick'em, I don't trick'em, Dime or nickel'em. The harvest is plentiful, so I just kick it with'em. Accidental, confidential, over Joey's instrumental witness how the Holy Spirit bless my mental.

HOOK:

I want some saints that'll stay vexed. Satan want we to die, but not yet. I gotsta be all that I'm called to be, a supernatural being, I'm a carry it like Jesus Christ the King.

2 VERSE:

I'm chosen out of the world that's why the world hatin me. So I stay vexed until the return of Jesus Christ the King. And I sing a new song and give thanks point blank, Satan get spanked, get thrown in the holding tank. As he walks the plank into the lake of fire, I should spit in his face, but why, he's expired. Nomore sin for hire. No more innocent kids caught up in crossfire. No disease poverty or unrighteous desire. In my prosperity I said I shall never be moved. Satin disapprove, ain't got no power here dude. I tried to told ya. Now I gots to shake the dust off my feet, I'm a Souljah. The saints go marching that's where I'll be.

HOOK:

I want some saints that'll stay vexed. Satan want we to die, but not yet. I gotsta be all that I'm called to be, a supernatural being, I'm a carry it like Jesus Christ the King.

Verse 3:

So I've been running my mouth for years now, that should tell you how I really feel about a coward. Have some respect for my God. I can show how. But God loves you so much, He'll let you work it out. I'm gonna show you what's up. Oh yes I drink from his cup, I am the sound of thunder. Demons can't stomach the come up, no beef. I'm eating chicken shawarma and hummus. St. Carter ain't dealing wit Gomer. I'm call to go kamikaze and I'm on it. The Son of God takes the stage He created. Who's the goner. Who's your lawyer. Lust of the flesh. Lust of the eyes. The pride of life. Strategic weapons used against Christ. The shelf-life won't be long, Satan know this, that's why he wants to share his abyss. That's why I hate evil so much, I can only do so much. Won't force my beliefs on ya, that's kinda cruel, plus it's rude, Jesus Christ my dude, died for all not just a few, me and my crew, we proof, everything we say about God is the truth. Either you dribble or shoot, bbq or mildew you gonna have to decide on a side or you've chosen. Men, women, and children. We won't be sinless, but the plan is to sin less

HOOK:

I want some saints that'll stay vexed. Satan want we to die, but not yet. I gotsta be all that I'm called to be, a supernatural being, I'm a carry it like Jesus Christ the King.

Luke 22:29-35

29 And I confer on you a kingdom, just as my Father conferred one on me, **30** so that you may eat and drink at my table in my kingdom and sit on thrones, judging the twelve tribes of Israel.

31 "Simon, Simon, Satan has asked to sift all of you as wheat. **32** But I have prayed for you, Simon, that your faith may not fail. And when you have turned back, strengthen your brothers."

WHAT INSPIRED ME TO WRITE SATAN WANT WE TO DIE

Yes Sirrr, tried to take me out. My mother, Katherine Davis White died when I was 4. So there went the nurturing. Not gonna go all into it but sin had a major part to do with it. Not her sin but another. She died of internal bleeding. Don't wanna speak on this anymore, let's keep going.

I'm in high school and I'm drinking, smoking that loud, dropping acid. Stealing fresh gear from shopping malls. Stealing liquor from liquor stores. All I'm saying is if I had my mom, she would have peeped what I was into and maybe could have made a difference in my daily.

Check it, we in the park drinking and getting high before the basketball game. Now we ain't feeling no pain and we ready to bounce but my car won't start. Now it's dark out and me & Bear looking at the engine. So Bear has a lighter in his hands an I'm checking to see if there's water in the battery. I grab Bear's hand with the lighter in it and pull it down so I can see if there's water in there, pow! Battery blows up in my face and I'm blind. Everybody strait tripping. They take me home to my father, Russell White who wants to take me to the hospital. I'm blind, all I see are stars. I told him no, I just wanna go to bed. In my mind I know I've been doing wrong. Don't know much about the Bible, not a spiritual kid, but I know I've been living the wrong way. So I told him to take me in the morning if I couldn't see then. I remember praying that night and in the morning I could see.

    Once I was driving from Charlotte NC to Augusta GA to pick up some money from a guy selling weed for me. Quentin in the backseat smoking dope. We been up for three days partying and making money. So I'm on cruise control rolling down 77 or 85, can't remember. Anyway, Quentin sleep in the backseat, suppose to be keeping me woke. So I'm sleep at the wheel on cruise control doing 60mph and I drift into a huge trench on the side of the road flying. Then the car shakes a little and I wake up in the trench getting it. I don't panic, put my foot on the break and slowed down then drove back on the road. Three seconds longer and we would have went airborne onto the other highway below us. We just made the bridge.

    I could go on and on with these stories of how the enemy orchestrated situations to take me out which I guess I'll do in another book. I've stomped from Portland Maine to the Florida Keys. Canada to Mexico. All I can tell you without looking in the book (BIBLE) is when sin is full grown, it equals death. Don't let Satan play you cause he's a major player. Relentless in his attack. We must be also. Everything I've done to hurt will be swallowed up by the love I've passed out over the years as a Christian and the love I continuously give now.

BALM IN GILEAD

1verse

I gotta stay true to this Christ life. Forever changed my life. Couldn't see it at first, but now I see past the Earth. True story. In 2000, April 23 I went flat line. No sunshine. Not coming back this time. Last thought on my mind. Literally. Out of options. One way to stop sin. But I wanna live. Death the unstoppable force. But can we hold it off. My life a coin toss. Who can I call to set it off. JESUS. Heal me O Lord and I shall be healed; save me O Lord and I shall be saved. For you are my praise, show me your ways, stronger each day. My mind is transformed and I'm saved. Where I'm from other cats might have been my influence. But my main influence was how I was doing it. Now my influence is the truest that ever did it. No one can deny, I laugh at your feelings. There is a Balm in Gilead

Epileptic Son near the towns of Caesarea Philippi, this just some of Jesus healing magnified.

The man with the withered hand, numerous blind men, woman with the issue of blood at Capernaum. Peter's Mother-in-law sick with a fever, Roman Centurion's paralyzed servant and the ten lepers in between the cities Samaria and Galilee the world would start to see just who Jesus Christ be. I am the Lord who heals you. He healed them all. He heals all our diseases. Youth is renewed like the Eagles wings. There was not a feeble one among all their tribes. Verse 37, Psalms 105. True story, not a man that should lie. Lazarus died, raised from the grave it happened. Mary Magdalene healed of evil spirits and infirmities cast out. No doubt. Ask Karen Clark Sheard if Jesus Christ got clout.

Jeremiah 8:19-22
Listen to the cry of my people from a land far away: "Is the Lord not in Zion? Is her King no longer there?"
"Why have they aroused my anger with their images,

with their worthless foreign idols?" "The harvest is past, the summer has ended, and we are not saved." Since my people are crushed, I am crushed;

I mourn, and horror grips me. Is there no balm in Gilead? Is there no physician there? Why then is there no healing

for the wound of my people?

WHAT INSPIRED ME TO WRITE BALM IN GILEAD

Power! The pure power of this song. The truth cause I've lived it, seen it, witnessed it over and over again even in my own life. If I've said it once, I've said it a thousand times. Heal me O Lord and I shall be healed. Save me O Lord and I shall be save. For you are my praise, show me your ways, stronger each day, I am what I am by God's grace.

Balm is simply medication used in the Bible day and still to this day. It's rubbed on the body to soothe and heal, simple and plain the majority of your pain.

Jesus, Jesus, Jesus. That's all I can say. You talking to a guy that has been diagnosed with an Enlarged Heart, Bad Kidneys, and Congestive Heart Failure to start. That was over 17 years ago so don't tell me there's not a balm in Gilead cause it is and His name is Jesus. That's right. Jesus has been faithful in healing me, adding days onto my life even when I wasn't faithful.

AMENNNN

I'm a take a swim on the deep end holding my breath like a dolphin. I'm all in.

Amennnn

Jesus did it again, forever keeping it trill, paid my $91,000 hospital bill.

Amennnn

Heard you in a coffin coughing. Thought I'd intervene, I'm seen snatching demons often.

Amennnn

This not in the natural, gottcha, 007 I'll attack you. Whole armor of God for da squad no forsod. Amennn

Got spiritual weapons, always test'em. Spiritual wickedness in high places. No flesh and blood, principalities, leave'em casualties.

Amennnn

Demons are dreaming but just so there's no misunderstanding these are nightmares, nighttime in the ocean, no boat, no flares.

Amennnn

If the sky cracked and it peeled back everything you've ever known under attack. No clap back. Them there's facts.

Amennnn

Red, brown, white, black now they interact, everybody diplomat. The end of times, you ever thought of that.

Amennn

What made me wanna write a song about that. Sometimes I go deep just ain't no coming back.

Amennnn

It's always gonna be big up God you can bet, with or without a check I sow into myself.

Amennnn

Im topshelf, till death do us part. I'll leave the field when I have nothing left or a stopped heart.

Amennnn

Our human bodies are perishable, dishonorable, and weak, all due to sin. It's like ignorance was built in.

Amennnn

Our glorified bodies will be imperishable, honorable, and powerful all due to Him. Something special can't get in a gym.

Amennnn

If we confess our sins, he is faithful and just to forgive our sins, and cleanse us from all unrighteousness, can I get an amen.

Amennnn

Revelation 7:12

saying: "**Amen**! Praise and glory and wisdom and thanks and honor and power and strength be to our God for ever and ever. **Amen**!"

WHAT INSPIRED ME TO WRITE AMENNNN

1 Cr 12:21-And the eye cannot say unto the hand, I have no need of thee: nor again the head to the feet, I have no need of you. The old hymn can't say to gospel hip hop I have no need of you. I know you might be getting up in the years, you a seasoned christian and the whole 9. But check this out. Sometimes when you rolling through and you see the neighborhood cats chilling' and you knew them when they was pups, roll your window down and pump some of that christian hip hop. Lets brake that barrier and keep that bridge up. You've been saved for 30+ years, prove it. I CHALLENGE every saint, every blood brought believer to go to a record store or download a christian hip hop cd. Buy one and have one in your music collection. It might plant a seed of righteousness where another might water. Then the Almighty God, creator of Heaven and Earth can bring the increase. Please pass this along!!! Amen! AMENNNN!

TRYIN' TO REACH YA

I'm a man of the people, dere it is. A friend will tell you the hard stuff, it's hard love sent from above.

1 verse: I speak to the world, I tell them the unpopular. For those that have ears to hear, the gates of hell not stopping ya. My minds made up how I'm gone live my life. Christ died for me now I die for Christ. Never was a follower, follow no man, unless it's God in the form of man. Didn't walk but I ran. Pay attention, my intention, not to mention my condition that has changed sense I've been saved. Dodging the grave, the devil gets played. All in the name of Jesus. Official in every season. I'm still grieving cause most don't get it, I'm committed

CHOURS

I'm a man of the people, dere it is. The sky is gonna crack, gotta deal wit that.

I'm a man of the people, dere it is. A friend will tell you the hard stuff, it's hard love sent from above.

2 verse:

Take a deep breath clear your mind cause this moment in time is your time, nobody else. Now you really going for self. So choose this day you rolling wit God or the devil. Choose this day, tomorrow ain't promised I betcha, wish you made a choice cause a gray area is a choice and the result of that choice is terror. Y'all can shine me on if you want to I'll still write these songs, God is longsuffering but don't take to long.

CHOURS

I'm a man of the people, dere it is. The sky is gonna crack, gotta deal wit that.

I'm a man of the people, dere it is. A friend will tell you the hard stuff, it's hard love sent from above.

3 verse:

Run run get around, I get around. 619 San Diego is my town. I puts it down like a tweeker chasing, that's my zeal, souls being turned over to Satan, not while I'm here. A concealed weapon at times I gotta stick and move. Just TRYIN to reach ya, do what I gotta do to warn ya. But won't press the issue to the point that I diss you, I am not that guy dude. Definitely not Mr.Softy, I can cut it, I battle principalities where you at cousin.

CHOURS

I'm a man of the people, dere it is. The sky is gonna crack, gotta deal wit that.

I'm a man of the people, dere it is. A friend will tell you the hard stuff, it's hard love sent from above.

Revelation 5

[*The Scroll and the Lamb*] Then I saw in the right hand of him who sat on the throne a scroll with writing on both sides and sealed with seven seals. And I saw a mighty angel proclaiming in a loud voice, "Who is worthy to break the seals and open the scroll?" But no one in heaven or on earth or under the earth could open the scroll or even look inside it.

WHAT INSPIRED ME TO WRITE TRYIN' TO REACH YA

    Jesus. Jesus inspired me. Jesus said to them, "The kings of the Gentiles lord it over them; and those who exercise authority over them call themselves Benefactors. But you are not to be like that. Instead, the greatest among you should be like the youngest, and the one who rules like the one who serves. For who is greater, the one who is at the table or the one who serves? Is it not the one who is at the table? But I am among you as one who serves. You are those who have stood by me in my trials. And I confer on you a kingdom, just as my Father conferred one on me, so that you may eat and drink at my table in my kingdom and sit on thrones, judging the twelve tribes of Israel. "Simon, Simon, Satan has asked to sift you as wheat. But I have prayed for you, Simon, that your faith may not fail. And when you have turned back, strengthen your brothers." It is what it is, "No Excuse". Jesus Himself intercedes on our behalf so our faith may not fail. You will turn back, its a matter of time. Now if your rebellious, that's the flip side. That's what stops everything and you don't apply. I wish I had more time to stress to you your power over your life and how you can and do effect other lives. Jesus has given you the greatest gift since life, eternal life. Let's tell as many as we can. Help me reach'em.

JESUS IS KING

CHOURS

Jesus is King, every knee will bow. Jesus is King, reigns without a doubt, eternally. The planet earth is soon to see who **is** the faithful witness, firstborn from the dead, freed us from our sins, Jesus is King.

1verse:

Ancient of days, all in a day's work, no negations, control your situation for the duration. If that was over your head, it's cool, the carnal mind ain't got a clue what to do, or what I said, they enemies of God don't be mislead. That's my nugget to you to escape damnation. I'll need your concentration, I'll explain His greatness. Love is salvation. It's being offered, won't you take it. Figured that much, if you was concentrating you'd be in a rush. Everything in you would cry out and say I've had enough. I bet a list of stuff, kinda hard to be true when you so cool.

CHOURS

Jesus is King, every knee will bow. Jesus is King, reigns without a doubt, eternally. The planet earth is soon to see who is the faithful witness, firstborn from the dead, freed us from our sins, Jesus is King.

2verse:

I guess it was a breakthrough from the first verse, you concentrated, you consecrated, you God's love. The life of God being poured out of vessels that have received the Fountains of living waters, overthrowing borders. A plan out of His nature, love and compassion for His creation. Bringing forth a Sonship company, allocation. The wicked will be destroyed out of the land, but God's ways aren't our ways and I understand. You can stab, shoot, poison, so many ways to destroy'em. The best way to make a friend is make that enemy a friend cause you know them. Now you've lost an enemy gained a friend. Both of y'all can benefit by this. I call it Jesus Theory.

CHOURS

Jesus is King, every knee will bow. Jesus is King, reigns without a doubt, eternally. The planet earth is soon to see who **is** the faithful witness, firstborn from the dead, freed us from our sins, Jesus is King.

Close: Mercy is full, so is His Grace. Mercy is full, worthy to be praised. Mercy is full, so is His grace. Jesus is king. Jesus is king. Jesus is king.

Revelation 17:14
They will wage war against the Lamb, but the Lamb will triumph over them because he is Lord of lords and **King** of **king**s—and with him will be his called, chosen and faithful followers."

Revelation 19:16
On his robe and on his thigh he has this name written: **king** of **king**s and lord of lords.

Revelation 1:5
and from Jesus Christ, who is the faithful witness, the firstborn from the dead, and the ruler **of** the **king**s of the earth. To him who loves us and has freed us from our sins by his blood,

WHAT INSPIRED ME TO WRITE JESUS IS KING

Millions of people aren't saved from sin cause of misinformation. People are saved (and get to go to heaven) by believing that Jesus is the Christ and putting their faith in Him. Asking Him to come in their hearts and forgive them of their sins. Baptism alone does not save. It does however make a statement to every molecule in existence that you ride and die with Jesus Christ. (When you die with Jesus, you will live with Jesus) It's His blood alone that does the saving, you really need to know this.

Revelation 1:5

and from Jesus Christ, who is the faithful witness, the firstborn from the dead, and the ruler of the kings of the earth. To him who loves us and has freed us from our sins by his blood... Now let's go to the water so we can touch the world and they might see what's on the inside of us from the outside. Glory be to God!

And there arose a great storm of wind, and the waves beat into the ship, so that it was now full. And he was in the hinder part of the ship, asleep on a pillow: and they awake him, and say unto him, Master, carest thou not that we perish? (do you even care if we die in this perfect storm when we know you have the power to control the elements?) And he arose, and rebuked the wind, and said unto the sea, Peace, be still. And the wind ceased, and there was a great calm. And he said unto them, Why are ye so fearful? how is it that ye have no faith? And they feared exceedingly, and said one to another, What manner of man is this, that even the wind and the sea obey him?

    This is who I'm rollin' with so now I practice sleeping in the storm. I practice faith in God. I practice gifts of the Spirit. I practice being anointed with the Spirit. I'm baptized in the Holy Spirit but not in all fullness yet, but when I am, lookout cause Jesus is King.

TO KNOW ME IS TO KNOW ME

CHOURS

Taking you back to the child that you might know the man. Peter Pan, Aqua Man, 007, the kingdom of heaven is at hand.

When I was a child, I spake as a child, I understood as a child, I thought as a child: but when I became a man, I put away childish thangs. Y'all gone know His name.

1verse:

I'm just a snot nose on my way to grandma Mag's house. 5 kids in the car, impossible for me to shut my mouth. Ma Ruth turned around an I tapped out. Yea she slapped me in my grill, I was so embarrass but I kept it trill at a young age. The Catholic school kid in the hood wit wild heads. Baptist church ever Sunday, Harry Davis White love God, Russell William White was a Don, where I'm from. Katherine Davis White died when I was 4, I told y'all before on Opportunity, you gotta pick a side there is no immunity. Hey, I'm just putting it out there that you might snatch it, come up outta there.

CHOURS

Taking you back to the child that you might know the man. Peter Pan, Aqua Man, 007, the kingdom of heaven is at hand.

When I was a child, I spake as a child, I understood as a child, I thought as a child: but when I became a man, I put away childish thangs. Y'all gone know His name.

2 verse:

It's important when you hear my name you know what I stand for. Yea I'm a nobody, see He must increase. That's what I stand for. I demand more of Him in my life cause I'm grown, I need resources, to obtain this level that I'm on and the level that I'm going. It's impossible for you to understand when your not knowing. It's like you always gotta go through hell and high water to see the morning. No performing, everything is real from my heartbeat to the breakbeat. I didn't choose this life on second thought I did choose this life, and this life chose me.

CHOURS

Taking you back to the child that you might know the man. Peter Pan, Aqua Man, 007, the kingdom of heaven is at hand.

When I was a child, I spake as a child, I understood as a child, I thought as a child: but when I became a man, I put away **childish** thangs. Y'all gone know His name.

3 verse:

The grown man is hear but until I disappear then reappear in a glorified form, keep them headphones on. Just before the dawn we gone conquer, no weapon against will prosper, no force will stop us. Our resources are eternal, and it don't stop. A man among boys from the bottom to the top. It's funny how money can make you immature, your a grown man, doing childish things, should have the mind of a king. How can fam depend on you. You far from God that's gonna cost. He's the boss. Everything you have will be lost.

CHOURS

Taking you back to the child that you might know the man. Peter Pan, Aqua Man, 007, the kingdom of heaven is at hand.

When I was a child, I spake as a child, I understood as a child, I thought as a child: but when I became a man, I put away childish thangs. Y'all gone know His name.

1 Corinthians 13:9-12

9 For we know in part and we prophesy in part, **10** but when completeness comes, what is in part disappears. **11** When I was a child, I talked like a child, I thought like a child, I reasoned like a child. When I became a man, I put the ways of childhood behind me. **12** For now we see only a reflection as in a mirror; then we shall see face to face. Now I know in part; then I shall know fully, even as I am fully known.

WHAT INSPIRED ME TO WRITE TO KNOW ME IS TO KNOW ME

Have you or do you feel like you are losing. Every time you turn around it's another bill or bad situation. Like your losing and can't win for nothing. Yea things can get worse but they're pretty bad now, right. Well look at yourself and speak to yourself, I will not give up. Flip the script on your emotions and tell God I'm not complaining. You've been so good to me and you'll see me out of this one also. If you don't know God or believe God is who he says he is, this might not be for you. But if you know God, act like you know God, real talk. You know how he is, he lives in the impossible. When you know all avenues are shutdown and can't be open by man, you go to God. Practice it fam. Don't let something scare you so bad you forget to call on the Most High God. Somebody needs to hear this right now so please take it and run with it. JUST DESCRIBING MYSELF

WILD HORSES

OPEN

Holding on tight to His everlasting arm, my mind is made up in His refuge I'll stay. Wild horses can't drag me away. A pack of wild horses can't drag me away.

1verse:

I have a theory that I'd like to share, sin is so easy we all need help. So when we do we have an advocate with the Father, Jesus Christ the righteous one. We should no longer be slaves to sin. If you hear these words and agree then say amen.

CHOURS

Holding on tight to His everlasting arm, my mind is made up in His refuge I'll stay. Wild horses can't drag me away. A pack of wild horses can't drag me away.

BRIDGE:

Jesus the Son, Son of Man. Gave His life for ransom, for all human Jesus tha King, King of Kings. Every knee will bow, every being see.

Father forgive, forgive our sins, through my words can I make amends. Father I love, love your ways. Cause you gave, that I'd receive grace.

2verse:

These are hard times you know by now, you been deceived if you've just found out. The Devil wants to accuse, still, kill, and destroy you. Jesus came that you may have life, have life to the fullness in time and out of time.

CHOURS

Holding on tight to His everlasting arm, my mind is made up in His refuge I'll stay. Wild horses can't drag me away. A pack of wild horses can't drag me away.

BRIDGE

Jesus the Son, Son of Man. Gave His life for ransom, for all human

Jesus tha King, King of Kings. Every knee will bow, every being see. Father forgive, forgive our sins, through my words can I make amends. Father I love, love your ways. Cause you gave, that I'd receive grace.

CLOSE

Holding on tight to His everlasting arm, my mind is made up in His refuge I'll stay. Wild horses can't drag me away. A pack of wild horses can't drag me away.

Romans 8:36-39

36 As it is written, For thy sake we are killed all the day long; we are accounted as sheep for the slaughter.

37 Nay, in all these things we are more than conquerors through him that loved us.

38 For I am persuaded, that neither death, nor life, nor angels, nor principalities, nor powers, nor things present, nor things to come,

39 Nor height, nor depth, nor any other creature, shall be able to separate us from the love of God, which is in Christ Jesus our Lord.

WHAT INSPIRED ME TO WRITE WILD HORSES

    This is my foundation. I grew up on this. Nobody made me it was just a drawing to the Word. It's like my spirit knew He was good to me long before I knew. Sometimes I wonder what people think cause I love Jesus so much. But then I know when you are drowning in the impossible (nothing created can help you) and you call on the name of Jesus, things change. It brings me to tears how good He's been to me.

    "Love suffers long and is kind; love does not envy; love does not parade itself, is not puffed up; does not behave rudely, does not seek its own, is not provoked, thinks no evil; does not rejoice in iniquity, but rejoices in the truth; bears all things, believes all things, hopes all things, endures all things. Love never fails. And now abide faith, hope, love, these three; but the greatest of these is love." I gave this message to you in part because we love in part. It's like we can't phantom what love is. We say real love or true love, but the fact of the matter is love is love. It's a simple word but one of the most powerful words in our existence. Before you tell someone you love them, read 1 Corinthians 13:1-13. If you really love someone shouldn't you be honest with them and yourself. Isn't that worth 3 minutes to read 13 verses to get a clear understanding on an expression you are about to reveal to someone you have about them. When you love, you are ready to die for that which you love and Wild Horses can't drag you away.

SUCKER FREE

Two years ago a friend of mine asked me to say some righteous. So I said this rhyme that I'm about to say. It gave God praise and it went this way. Jesus Christ bless me on the microphone. Raised me from the dead when my mind was gone. The cul-de-sac Colfax my part time home. Repentance is a weapon used to atone.

Samson killed thousands with a jawbone. Sucker demons is an undertone. Ankle biters, that's more at home. But in the name of Jesus to the wind there thrown. My faith stand alone and that's set in stone. My purpose is to let God's will be known. Jesus on the right hand side of the thrown. Until the sky cracks all creation groans. Sucker demons stay in your zone. Spiritual warfare, I want you gone. So I pray without ceasing, I really mean it. God on my mind right or wrong I believe Him to be more than a conquer. I not stopping ya. This my opinion, my faith, I've been saved by grace. So when I see Him face to face, don't know what I'll do. Just long as He says well done my good and faithful servant, cool.

Galatians 2:4
4 This matter arose because some false believers had infiltrated our ranks to spy on the freedom we have in Christ Jesus and to make us slaves.

1 Corinthians 2:16
For who hath known the mind of the Lord, that he may instruct him? but we have the **mind of Christ**.

WHAT INSPIRED ME TO WRITE SUCKER FREE

For beginners, you might have to know a little about Hip Hop to feel me on this one. All I'm sayin' is that this world is hard. Like Precise say it's a crap shoot. We've been desensitized meaning the tv, radio, media says anything and shows anything and it's cool. But if you preach Christ Jesus they want to shut you down. This is in the streets and a lot of churches. Y'all got your own opinion cool, write about it. All I know is cats dying and going to hell by the seconds and God say's His word will not return void. We need to get together and get it in. You cats that got the money and resources and trying to hold on tight, what you have will be taken from you, watch. All my saints spreading the goodnews of Jesus Christ, stay encourage and Sucker Free.

SPIRIT STORMIN' IN ME

Pastor Charles:

Too, too renew minds oh Lord. We pray for a renewing of the mind this morning. We pray Lord that you would bless us with a heart oh God that says I will stand, I will not bend. I will not bow. I will stand and walk with you. I will stand firm in Jesus name. I will stand for righteousness, I will not go back and forth, I will stand for that which is right that I know pleases God.

First verse:

Unsearchable riches, more than you can stand. My flow is of spirit not of man. Holla if you hear me. Preach peace while in the form of man. Come among you as gentile as I can. Knowing all the while you'll treat me like the Son of Man. But I won't stop spreading the gospel throughout the land. Everything I do I'm lifting up His name, I don't expect you to understand unless your saved. Them nonbelievers, they think I won't make a dent. So much evidence, past tense, present tense, future tense. People dying for biblical sense, my heart's content. Dear Heavenly Father widen my tent. I'm convinced your presence will present more than dollars and cents. More than soul out events, salvation for souls hell bent. Believers, seek ye first the Kingdom of God and it's righteousness. Press to posses in great faith, nothing less. And all these things shale be added unto you. His promises, and everything He said He'd do. I said everything He said He'd do.

CHOURS

Spirit storming in me, performing transforming in me, conforming a heartwarming pouring of peace.

Spirit storming in me, performing transforming in me, conforming a heartwarming pouring of peace.

Second verse:

I receive not the spirit of the world, but the Spirit which is of God, that I might know the things that's freely given to me of God. So I'm set apart, vital part, fresh start. No condemnation homes so don't reminisce that hard heart. Honor shall uphold the humble in spirit. I pray to God daily the power that I submit. Satan on the blitz, but I'm in God's palm, can't be snatch out. So tell me the outcome. Can't fight the enemy by myself but I see they're on the fritz. He that is joined unto the Lord is one spirit. God is a spirit, worship Him in spirit and in truth. So soon the moment of truth for the old and the youth. A downpour of spiritual blessings got me prepared for spiritual war. That's what I stand for, I die for. Need I say more. Filthy rich or dirt poor, accusers uncalled for. Neither do I condemn thee. Go sin no more. That's what Jesus said when He was drawing in the dirt. He looked up and He said, GO SIN NOMORE.

CHOURS

Spirit storming in me, performing transforming in me, conforming a heartwarming pouring of peace.

Spirit storming in me, performing transforming in me, conforming a heartwarming pouring of peace.

Third verse:

Who is a God like unto thee that pardon iniquity, set the captives free in the mind or under lock and key. He that is not wit me is against me, woman thou art loosed from thine infirmities. Thou art ever with me and all that I have is thine. You'll resign with the Devine that's the bottom line. Arise, go thy way, thy faith have made thee whole. Taring down strongholds from sin sick souls, He's faithful. Receive thy sight thou faith have saved thee, be grateful. For the Son of Man has come seek and save which was lost. Thank God for that and the day of Pentecost. Now go show yourself unto to the priest, peace be with you. I'm taking His word to the streets from the church pews. I die daily. The power of the blood the enemy could not diminish. So thankful, so thankful, so thankful Christ said it is finished. Hallelujah! I'm so thankful Jesus Christ said "It is finished"

CLOSING

X4: Spirit storming in me, performing transforming in me, conforming a heartwarming pouring of peace.

Pastor Charles:

Have a spark of inspiration, that you can be this, that you can be that. And the enemy sees that and he'll make you feel less than you are. He'll make you think that you never will become that and that's a lie straight out of the pit of hell! And we're standing up to tell him, that is a lie! We're standing up to tell him I don't have to keep using dope! I don't have to keep drinking! I don't have to keep living in immorality! I am free from that, in the name of the Lord Jesus! And I intend to walk with God! I intend to be all that God has called me to be. Amen! Amen! We're taking authority! The God given authority over the enemy and the wilds, the strategies, the design of the enemy in our lives.

Luke 11:13
If you then, though you are evil, know how to give good gifts to your children, how much more will your Father in heaven give the **Holy Spirit** to those who ask him!"

John 14:26
But the Advocate, the **Holy Spirit**, whom the Father will send in my name, will teach you all things and will remind you of everything I have said to you.

WHAT INSPIRED ME TO WRITE SPIRIT STORMIN' IN ME

R I P Erika and all the others that went before you that are in Christ Jesus. There is no condemnation in Jesus so you will never see hell. John 11:25 Jesus said to her, "I am the resurrection and the life. The one who believes in me will live, even though they die.. 1 John 1:9 If we confess our sins, he is faithful and just to forgive us our sins, and to cleanse us from all unrighteousness....So if we do one thing - confess our sins, God will do 4 things - 1)Be faithful to us. 2)Be just with us.

3)Forgive us our sins. 4)cleanse from all unrighteousness. Remember God is Holy and this (1 John 1:9) makes fellowship possible with God squashing unforgiveness and unrighteousness gaining a mansion in the Kingdom.

For as many as are led by the Spirit of God, they are the sons of God. For ye have not received the spirit of bondage again to fear; but ye have received the Spirit of adoption, whereby we cry, Abba, Father. The Spirit itself beareth witness with our spirit, that we are the children of God:

Galatians 4:6-7 And because ye are sons, God hath sent forth the Spirit of his Son into your hearts, crying, Abba, Father. Wherefore thou art no more a SERVANT, but a SON; and if a son, then an heir of God through Christ...... Don't get it twisted, this is only when God says so. Check it. The one who doesn't work for price or reward, and that is a son. The servants work for their price. They get their rewards, and there are rewards for those who work. The servants expect pay for their work but the son doesn't work for pay because he is working for his own property. The kingdom that belongs to his father also belongs to him. He works because he loves the kingdom and his father.

TAKE ON ME

1st VERSE

This was the first invite from Christ, I'm dropping jewels in your life. Come unto me, and I'm a show ya free. Come unto me all ye that labor and are heavy laden, and I will give you rest, dismiss the stress, give you power above the rest. I will spill blood for you to be blessed, put me to the test. Let me in your chest. I'll show you things you never seen before and when this life is over, I'm a show you more. Sovereign to the core. I am Christ the Lord. And if any man sin I am the advocate with the Father. Not only you, throughout the world, regardless. Seems like no hope at all, everything we love don't have to be gone (Take Me On)

CHORUS

Arms open wide, today is the day you learn how to fly. It's only right that I rep Christ the author and finisher of my life. Taught me how to fight. I got a burden to expedite this truth to you, no matter who say it ain't cool. They words turn to drool. There breath turns to vapor, this is the season for takin'em out. Christ gave us the route and resources. We don't do it, we made our choices, He gave us the Keys (Take On Me)

2nd VERSE

Convinced that'll you'll die for this cake and it's heavy, the truth is scary. The Father's will is none should be barred under those circumstances. Enhance your chances for the better conditions, apply what you're listening. This song in particular, will you except the mission. See if any man be in Christ, he is a new creature, old things are passed away, behold all things are become new. This is what I'm trying to get across to you. But secular got you fooled. Poverty is far beyond the absence of jewelry, cash and whatever. I want you to be blessed today and be blessed forever. Not temporary, we are the sons and daughters, daughters and sons (Take Me On)

CHORUS

Arms open wide, today is the day you learn how to fly. It's only right that I rep Christ the author and finisher of my life. Taught me how to fight. I got a burden to expedite this truth to you, no matter who say it ain't cool. They words turn to drool. There breath turns to vapor, this is the season for takin'em out. Christ gave us the route and resources, we don't do it, we made our choices. He gave us the Keys (Take On Me)

3rd VERSE

As far as I can see men are not united, but that don't matter, all are invited. I look at the sky's above and I thank God I ain't who I was. I had to come like this that you might see His love. So if you're thirsty take a drink cuz. This be the water of life and it's always free. You are what you drink. So many people don't understand God, let's put it out there. We all were born in sin, we all started backwards. He is faithful and just to forgive me of my sins, cleanse me of all unrighteousness. That's as hard as it gets. Your gonna have to believe in the unseen to get back yours. It's called faith, the substance of things hoped for. Jesus is a new song, (Take Me On)

OUTTRO

Arms open wide, today is the day you learn how to fly. It's only right that I rep Christ the author and finisher of my life. Taught me how to fight. I got a burden to expedite this truth to you, no matter who say it ain't cool. They words turn to drool. There breath turns to vapor, this is the season for takin'em out. Christ gave us the route and resources. We don't do it, we made our choices. He gave us the Keys

Isaiah 14:25

I will crush the Assyrian in **my** land; on **my** mountains I will trample him down. His **yoke** will be **take**n from **my** people, and his burden removed from their shoulders."

Matthew 11:29
Take my yoke upon you and learn from me, for I am gentle and humble in heart, and you will find rest for your souls.

Matthew 16:19
And I will give unto thee the **keys** of the kingdom of heaven: and whatsoever thou shalt bind on earth shall be bound in heaven: and whatsoever thou shalt loose on earth shall be loosed in heaven.

Revelation 1:18
I am he that liveth, and was dead; and, behold, I am alive for evermore, Amen; and have the **keys** of hell and of death.

WHAT INSPIRED ME TO WRITE
TAKE ON ME

Sometimes we gotta start over with God. Yea we give our life to Christ and we go right back out and do the same stuff (milk redeemed) we did before we came to walk with Jesus.

If this is you, you feel like why did you say that prayer and ask Jesus into your heart and your right back out there in the mix. FREEZE. Don't move, don't think just listen...Jesus is faithful to forgive us of our sins and cleanse us of all unrighteousness. 1 John 1:9 If we confess our sins, he is faithful and just to forgive us our sins, and to cleanse us from all unrighteousness... You mess up, ask Jesus to clean you up. Stay in the Word. You mess up, ask Jesus to clean you up. Keep walking with Jesus. Stay in the Word. You mess up, ask Jesus to clean you up. You 6 months into your walk with The Lord, you feeling good, people and family members see a change in your inner appearance and your outter appearance. All of a sudden, you get thrown a curve ball. Something, whatever the case draws you away from Jesus. FREEZE. Don't think twice. Ask Jesus to clean you up. A big part of walking with Jesus is to walk with Jesus. Also when someone in Christ takes a fall, they don't start over mans way (back to start). Oh nooo, they start over God's way. God's way is where you fall off at is where you start. God is pleased when we ask Jesus to clean us up. God loves us so much I could break out in tears now. My heart hurts for the lost. We are called and we live with a purpose. We don't judge, we press and go hard in the paint that the world may know of God's unmeasurable love.

    Spiritual Warfare / Binding & Loosing. Matthew 18:18-20 Verily I say unto you, Whatsoever ye shall bind on earth shall be bound in heaven: and whatsoever ye shall loose on earth shall be loosed in heaven. Again I say unto you, That if two of you shall agree on earth as touching any thing that they shall ask, it shall be done for them of my Father which is in heaven. For where two or three are gathered together in my name, there am I in the midst of them......

Binding & loosing is a command! It is building the Church of God Almighty by moving into the devil's territory. Where do you think these souls came from? They have been held in captivity by the powers of darkness. After our Lord was crucified, He descended into the bowls of earth to preach to the captives held there by death; He took the keys from the devil, loosed the prisoners in 'Abraham's bosom'(refers to the place of comfort in sheol (Greek: hades) where the Jews said the righteous dead awaited Judgment Day) from captivity and then led them up to glory with Him. The Lord left us these keys to unlock the gates of hell and the authority in His name to continue the work of building His Church, "HIS CHURCH". We became solid living stones in that Church when we make use of the tools, His commandments, in our day by day experience. Then, we automatically begin to add to the church/ministry daily through augmenting these commands.

This is where the Kingdom of God begins to become a place where the redeemed of The Lord live; in righteousness, peace and joy in the Holy Ghost (Romans 14:17).

Begin to bind all the powers of darkness which come against you and loose all the powers of Heaven which are at your disposal, in the name of Jesus. Binding and loosing go together as the Word says! To bind is to bind something up so it can't move. To loose is to turn something loose. So bind the evil and loose the opposite, the greater powers of God-His fruits, His gifts, His ministering spirits , etc. "Greater is He that is in you, than he that is in the world" (1 John 4:4). These greater powers are those of God Almighty through His Holy Spirit dwelling in you . They dispel the powers of darkness.

CAN YOU HEAR ME NOW

OPENING

With da quickness, blessed with Joey and Quincy the gifted, overnight in fact, how sporadic is that. Man of God on attack, wins back to back, my cardio avoids cardiac. 007 the big payback. Seen and unseen try to hold me back, but I lack nothing. Evidence Jesus is coming. Will see who's the dummy. It ain't nothing funny cause I'm dead serious, you too near me not to be hearing this.

1st VERSE

This be the throwback a piece of who I was, things that I've done, my first love, the weed. I've had pounds you wouldn't believe. Buried so long mold formed on the leaves. I was so deceived. Cash came so fast I got robbed but I didn't got blast, thanks for the past. Now I see what God was screaming, He had to take me to death so I could get the meaning. I was dead as cement. The wages of sin is death. I don't care who you are, if you have breath left go for self. I dare you to conversant with the Father, tell Him why you're bothered, tell Him why you're fed up, tell a what you're missing, ask Him is He listening. Ask Him about money, tell Him to show you His ways. How you need a thousand fold blessing these days. God is not flawed He will come through and revived us, to whom much is given much is required.

CHOURS

With da quickness, blessed with Joey and Quincy the gifted, overnight in fact, how sporadic is that. Man of God on attack, wins back to back, my cardio avoids cardiac. 007 the big payback. Seen and unseen try to hold me back, but I lack nothing. Evidence Jesus is coming. Will see who's the dummy. It ain't nothing funny cause I'm dead serious, you too near me not to be hearing this.

2nd VERSE

Bon voyage, gear on mad camouflage at the travel lodge, dogging flying steal but can't dislodge, cause your gats clogged, a sabotage, where's your entourage when you need'em, now ya bleeding. Lead lodge in your leg, chest, arm. For what reason. Ease selector, rest yourself, you need a new season. How can I reach ya before all of this happens, I know you willing to die for da cream. Straight gangstas, Gun clappers. But a, don't you think ya hustling backwards. Lets do an analysis. What can we use? The Holy Bible kid. Seems like ungodly things to bring food to your table. World programed, like Cane killed Able. You'd kill for tv cable. I vision mad heads with warning labels. Most unstable. Hope you're looking for the savior. He gone run the universe, this the truth, and I'm a run it too.

OUTTRO

With da quickness, blessed with Joey and Quincy the gifted, overnight in fact, how sporadic is that. Man of God on attack, wins back to back, my cardio avoids cardiac. 007 the big payback. Seen and unseen try to hold me back, but I lack nothing. Evidence Jesus is coming. Will see who's the dummy. It ain't nothing funny cause I'm dead serious, you too near me not to be hearing this.

Romans 12:11
Never be **lacking** in zeal, but keep your spiritual fervor, serving the Lord.

1 Corinthians 16:17
I was glad when Stephanas, Fortunatus and Achaicus arrived, because they have supplied what was **lacking** from you.

Colossians 1:24

[*Paul's Labor for the Church*] Now I rejoice in what I am suffering for you, and I fill up in my flesh what is still **lacking** in regard to Christ's afflictions, for the sake of his body, which is the church.

1 Thessalonians 3:10
Night and day we pray most earnestly that we may see you again and supply what is **lacking** in your faith.

James 1:4
Let perseverance finish its work so that you may be mature and complete, not **lacking** anything.

WHAT INSPIRED ME TO WRITE
CAN YOU HEAR ME NOW

    My Mother in-law is 73 to 77 years young and has the heart of a lion. I miss her a lot cause she's in Oregon and I'm in San Diego. We talked the other day and she was telling me about all the destruction going on play by play because I was not near a tv or radio. She also told me more than one time,"tell'em Jesus is coming. Tell everybody Jesus is coming". I saw this on my yahoo page ("We have requested funeral homes across the nation to send us many body bags and coffins. But we simply don't have enough," he told the AP. "We just did not expect such a thing to happen. It's just overwhelming.") So I want to say Jesus is coming. I know you got your life and your routine but be true to yourself, Jesus is coming and when it happens it will be so fast you won't be able to do anything about. It's gonna happen just like that. Break yourself while you got a shot to. Don't matter if you got Will Smith money, get your house in order. Jesus is coming sooner than you think.

    And another thing, I'm lead by the Holy Spirit to snatch a yoke off of somebody to day and exchange it for power. Snatch a lie and exchange it for power. This decade we must stay focused. If you've made a change for a better future, stay the course. Let NOTHING separate you from the love of God and the plan He has written on your heart. A lot of folk might not agree and I care about them but I'm in the soul saving business. I'm in the exposing the lies from the pit of hell business. So if and they do so often tell you you're not connected with the Body of Christ cause you are not in a church or go to a church, don't receive that. Get in your word. Get Godly council. Talk to God often. Ask Him to order your steps. He will direct you to a Church or a Ministry or what ever He has for you as long as you keep your heart on Him. Don't just rush and join anything cause somebody telling you that you are not connected to Christ. I'm saying this and backing it up with God's Word so no one can twist what I write and even a child can understand this. FOCUSE

Romans 8:35, Who shall separate us from the love of Christ? shall tribulation, or distress, or persecution, or famine, or nakedness, or peril, or sword? Nothing! I'll let nothing separate me. Don't you let nothing separate you from the love of God. God bless all that read and receive this becoming leaders, not followers. Can you hear me now.

YA BLOOD

Singing Part)

Now that I trust an truly believe, that you came to make me free. Great He that lives in me. It's so cool, I can seek you diligently, dominion from sea to sea. You deliver me from in·iq·ui·ty

Your blood is apond me, wash my sins away. I present my body a living sacrifice, holy and exceptable,

A vessel that is willing,

A vessel that is willing,

A vessel that is willing.

Lord I just want to praise you for your Word.

Praise you for your Body,

Praise you for your Son that died.

He was crucified. For, your soul and for mine, to give sight to the blind. If you call on His name you shall be saved. That's my joy. Our bodies are the members of Christ. We got the armor of God to fight. In Jesus we have the Vic·to·ry. Your blood is apond me, wash my sins away. I present my body a living sacrifice, holy and exceptable,

A vessel that is willing,

A vessel that is willing,

A vessel that is willing.

Lord I just want to praise you for your Word.

Praise you for your Body,

Praise you for your Son that died.

He was crucified.

(Rap Part)

Lift your hands up like you know something.

00 put it down like it ain't nothing.

Turnup in the whip cause your bass humming.

Church, garage, the lodge, I ain't fronting.

Corner store, bodega, a little something, something,

Did I say put your hands down, keep'em up then.

God been to good, let'em know somethin'.

Do it by yourself, do it in public.

Got a gang of cousins, it's like that.

Hands to the sky, I'm talking all dat.

They love The Lord so much, how bout that.

They praying so much, I don't need a strap.

An I Christwalk no matter where I'm at.

Souljahs of Christ, yea I'm bout that.

Didn't come for the righteous but sinners to repentance.

He rains on the just and unjust, don't you get it.

(Singing Part)

Now that I trust an truly believe, that you came to make me free. Great He that lives in me. It's so cool, I can seek you diligently, dominion from sea to sea. You deliver me from in·iq·ui·ty

Your blood is apond me, wash my sins away. I present my body a living sacrifice, holy and exceptable,

A vessel that is willing,

A vessel that is willing,

A vessel that is willing.

Lord I just want to praise you for your Word.

Praise you for your Body,

Praise you for your Son that died.

He was crucified. For, your soul and for mine, to give sight to the blind. If you call on His name you shall be saved. That's my joy. Our bodies are the members of Christ. We got the armor of God to fight. In Jesus we have the Vic•to•ry. Your blood is apond me, wash my sins away. I present my body a living sacrifice, holy and exceptable,

A vessel that is willing,

A vessel that is willing,

A vessel that is willing.

Lord I just want to praise you for your Word.

Praise you for your Body,

Praise you for your Son that died.

He was crucified.

1 John 1:7
But if we walk in the light, as he is in the light, we have fellowship with one another, and the **blood of Jesus**, his Son, purifies us from all sin.

Revelation 1:5
and from **Jesus** Christ, who is the faithful witness, the firstborn from the dead, and the ruler **of** the kings **of** the earth. To him who loves us and has freed us from our sins by his **blood**,

Ephesians 2:13
But now in Christ **Jesus** you who once were far away have been brought near by the **blood of** Christ.

WHAT INSPIRED ME TO WRITE YA BLOOD

    You got a bucket-list and not rolling with Jesus Christ, you better put Him at the top of your list. I know we say that Jesus is the son of God. We learn this as children then we grow up to decide if we really believe or not. I'm talking to people that this applies to right now. Check this, what if you really believed Jesus died and came back to life. Not just talk but really believed and would tell anybody you believed this. The world has desensitized us and we accept things people of a royal priesthood would never except. If a man put himself in harms way for me and my fam and suffered and died cause of it, I owe that man something. I owe that man a lot. I owe that man my life. But here's the kicker, no that's the kicker. This is just more to it. He says it gives him joy to die for me and my family so we can live. He's like,"you don't owe me nothing, I did it so you would have a choice". So I think I could at least say thank you once a day, you know something in remembrance to what he has done for me. So I do. Thank you Jesus. I'm just that kinda guy to do that, that's all.

Justification, sanctification, glorification. Get in wit-da-quickness where you fit in and tell somebody. I'm in sanctification. I've been set apart and God is making me holy. It's hard, nobody said it would be easy. I'm hanging on everyday by the skin of my teeth talking to God asking for guidance, health, money, the whole nine. I can go to Him in Spirit and in Truth now cause I've been washed in His Blood. Using weapons he gave me like repentance, the mind of Christ, you know just talking to him. The big truckload of grace he gives me on the daily I give to others making some deadly situations turn into joyous times. Yea he justified me. Now he's sanctifying me. Look it up if you need more understanding of the word. One day soon he'll glorify me and it's on! All because of the Blood of Jesus.

BE NOBODYS FOOL

HOOK

Be nobody's fool, make it do what it do. Read the contract before you sign on the bottom line. Cause the bottom line is you got options son daughter. Business should be done decent and in order. Demons I slaughter, read between the lines. I'm longsuffering, but I'm not blind. Catch this nugget, another state on mind. Tomorrow ain't promised, that's the golden rule, be nobody's fool. Be nobody's foo1st: 007 yea I do this in remembrance

Of the one that died that You might receive forgiveness

Streets calling me and it's not like I don't hear'em

Yea I miss the cash and the grass and the @&$

But I'd rather be righteous, I'd rather be like Him

Than to be like you, another industry fool

Don't know what to do with all that cash, ain't got a clue

To whom much is given, to whom much is do

My dude what you sow gonna come back to you

Are you really ready for the consequences, cool

No matter who you are, no matter who you knew

Ask Christ in your heart, be nobody's fool

HOOK

Be nobody's fool, make it do what it do. Read the contract before you sign on the bottom line. Cause the bottom line is you got options son daughter. Business should be done decent and in order. Demons I slaughter, read between the lines. I'm longsuffering, but I'm not blind. Catch this nugget, another state on mind. Tomorrow ain't promised, that's the golden rule, be nobody's fool. Be nobody's fool.

2nd;

Got wit God go and get how I live it

I can show you hundred dollar bills up to the ceiling

I can show you supernatural power think I'm kidding

All this a add on, a comp for this living

Souljahs of Christ gonna blow like a blizzard

Demons gonna have to scatter homeboy it's written

This my grind, my time, my vision

That you be freed from that yoke you've been givin'

Take that trap change boi' make a legal billion

Take that trap change boi' make a legal billion

Take that trap change boi' make a legal billion

Cutdown killing innocent men, women, children

Wasting no time cause the clock gonna stop

Sanctification is the bottom to the top

If ya soul heard me this will suffice

Bring into captivity every thought to the obedience of Christ

HOOK

Be nobody's fool, make it do what it do. Read the contract before you sign on the bottom line. Cause the bottom line is you got options son daughter. Business should be done decent and in order. Demons I slaughter, read between the lines. I'm longsuffering, but I'm not blind. Catch this nugget, another state on mind. Tomorrow ain't promised, that's the golden rule, be nobody's fool. Be nobody's fool.

Matthew 7:7-12
Ask, Seek, Knock

7 "Ask and it will be given to you; seek and you will find; knock and the door will be opened to you. **8** For everyone who asks receives; the one who seeks finds; and to the one who knocks, the door will be opened. **9** "Which of you, if your son asks for bread, will give him a stone? **10** Or if he asks for a fish, will give him a snake? **11** If you, then, though you are evil, know how to give good gifts to your children, how much more will your Father in heaven give good gifts to those who ask him! **12** So in everything, do to others what you would have them do to you, for this sums up the Law and the Prophets.

WHAT INSPIRED ME TO WRITE BE NOBODYS FOOL

    The truth only has one meaning but so many applications. The truth will make you free. The truth will set you free. The truth hurts. You can't handle the truth. The truth and nothing but the truth and so on. We are in a world where the truth means everything and we wear transparent blindfolds and can't see a thing. The truth will move you to another state physically or another state of mind. A lie don't care who tells it and will let you swim in death until you drown. If I had know the truth when I was young, it's a good chance I wouldn't have this wire laid across my heart now. Families should have a time once a week when they get together for the purpose to tell the truth to each other in love. Only one truth per person to avoid conflict but to see a loved one prosper. If we say we family lets act like it an all of us prosper, let none be left behind. If you apply this it won't be easy I'm telling you now and that's the hard truth.

    My mother in law took me to see this apostle once. I'll never forget it. I'm not bringing any charges against him because I've grown in God's word. I did examine his spirit to the best of my ability. He talked about how he saved this business man millions of dollars cause he had the keys to the Kingdom. He asked for money. Thousands. He started out asking for $10,000. Wanted the people to raise there hand if they were gonna give the 10 G's. Some did. Then he went down the ladder, thousands then hundreds. Evil is flourishing in the camp and it doesn't have to be that way. I'm sitting there in the congregation with my bible and my finger on the scripture (THE TRUTH) while this person is on stage saying he'll give you the keys to the kingdom (for a fee) (yea I wish I didn't say that, but I did) so all these miraculous things can happen in your life and your business. What gets me is I'll show you that which you seek and much more at no charge. But then a man can come along and sell you a lie. Pastors, I ask you today to humble yourselves before God. I'm nobody but I can see. I'm praying for you leaders that have extravagant homes and people under you have no covering, homeless. I'm really asking pastors to love more. Leave the 99 and go get the one. Look your followers in the eyes. What's the Holy Spirit in you telling you of the continence on their face. We all most grow everyday in The Lord, no exceptions. So we have to make it known the things of God to His people and persuade them to be desperate for His word. I'll start right here cause of my story of the apostle having the keys. As a leader, I know a house divided against itself can not stand. So I examine and go as led by the Holy Spirit. This is the Holy Spirit leading me today, "Matthew 16:19 And I will give unto thee the keys of the kingdom of heaven: and whatsoever thou shalt bind on earth shall be bound in heaven: and whatsoever thou shalt loose on earth shall be loosed in heaven." In this book I've talked about bind and loose in depth. Be Nobody Fool!

WHERE YA AT?

God bless me to hold a few offices. But most of the time I feel I'm alone. Nobody feeling me. But I know that ain't the case still I find myself asking where's my support. Where's the Body of Christ? Then I look in the mirror.

(INTRO)

Where the Saints at? Where the Prophets at? Where the Souljahs at? Where the Christians at? The true worshipers. Where you at? Where you at? Where you at?

(1 VERSE 007)

I tell them Christian rap they laugh I tell them gospel rap they gasp for air, I see why they so so scared, growth, so I just humble myself no need to dis you. Speak life and the body of Christ must grow, but I'll continue. But remember, God spoke through a donkey if we don't praise Him the rocks will cry our. I can't let you shut my mouth. That's His word and this verse is for saints that don't believe it. I run across'em often, need more seeking need more reading scriptures like this one. Now has Christ risen from the grave and become the first fruits of them that slept, yelp. That's the word of God on this beat, strait scripture. God can use you to explain it to a youth or ignorant listener. For as in Adam all die, even so in Christ all shall be made alive. This the reason why I strive, cause Christ died and God raised Him up. You see where I'm going. Cause of Jesus death has no victory on me. Act like ya know me.

(CHORUS)

Where the Saints at? Waiting on The Lord, praising The Lord I've spoken. He keep all of His bones, not one is broken. Where the Prophets at? In the church in the streets, In the sons and daughters. Let all things be done decent and in order. Where the Souljahs at? Mighty men of valor. Virtuous women till they die. Under the authority of the Most High. Where the Christians at? The true worshipers. Where you at? Where you at? Where you at?

(2 VERSE

Having no hope in God, not gonna happen

Strangers to the covenant, not gonna happen

Rejecting the Holy Spirit, not gonna happen

Without Christ, no no no, not gonna happen

unconscious of who you are

This will not work, we are His workmanship created in Christ Jesus unto good works, which God has ordained before the foundations of the world, dominion is given amongst the living. Not the unforgiving. We talking major positions. So thankful I can get in where I fit in. Affairs of the universe type business. The harvest is plentiful I gots ta get it, to me it's a given, eternal living, something evil forces gotta deal with. That's the realness. Authority in this realm, cause I am with the great I am. Bringing God glory is my life, my legacy, my story. Make it your mission to play your position. Almighty God I adore you.

(CHORUS)

Where the Saints at? Waiting on The Lord, praising The Lord I've spoken. He keep all of His bones, not one is broken. Where the Prophets at? In the church in the streets, In the sons and daughters. Let all things be done decent and in order. Where the Souljahs at? Mighty men of valor. Virtuous women till they die. Under the authority of the Most High. Where the Christians at? The true worshipers. Where you at? Where you at? Where you at?

(3 VERSE 007)

Let's go a bit deeper. We among believers so we can kick it. Unbelievers listening in but really though who they kidding. The preaching of the Cross to them that parish is foolishness. This is a shot out to the filthy rich or average hooligan that ain't saved. We coming to get ya because of what Christ gave His life, presenting our bodies a living sacrifice. Holy acceptable unto God which is our reasonable service. Saints, Prophets. Souljahs no need to get nervous. We have the victory. We take the gospel from the pews to the streets. You know they hear us coming, we love whoever's slumming. Rich or poor, we intercede that's what we hear for.

Here's the proof. It ain't hard to find, it ain't hard to tell. We shall endure, we shall prevail. Oh yea. God didn't give us a spirit of fear but of power love a sound mind. This spiritual ware fare, right here, right here, right here.

(CHORUS)

(OUTRO)

Acts 8:20-23

20 Peter answered: "May your money perish with you, because you thought you could buy the gift of God with money! **21** You have no part or share in this ministry, because your heart is not right before God. **22** Repent of this wickedness and pray to the Lord in the hope that he may forgive you for having such a thought in your heart. **23** For I see that you are full of bitterness and captive to sin."

James 2:14-26

[*Faith and Deeds*] What good is it, my brothers and sisters, if someone claims to have faith but has no deeds? Can such faith save them? Suppose a brother or a sister is without clothes and daily food. If one of you says to them, "Go in peace; keep warm and well fed," but does nothing about their physical needs, what good is it?

WHAT INSPIRED ME TO WRITE WHERE YA AT?

You ever seen someone standing at a corner or at a store asking for change. I've seen people give them money, beer, joints, all type of stuff. What's funny is that a lot of Christians will not give a penny to that person. "Verily, verily, I say unto you, He that believe on me, the works that I do shall he do also; and greater works than these shall he do; because I go unto my Father. John 14:12" OK, lets test it. Lord bless that man begging for change. Let your will be done in his life, in Jesus name, amen. Lord bless that woman out there like that. Let your will be done in her life in the name of Jesus. We as Christians have the power and authority given by God to bless others. "Bless the LORD, O my soul: and all that is within me, bless his holy name. Psa 103:1"

I'm basically speaking to the Body of Christ. Something like a roll-call. A song so we don't sleep on the benefits, the power, the authority, and the ability to change lives. Practice 5 second, 10 second prayers all through your day out of your mouth or in your head for any and every need you see. Be a real blessing. People are depending on us and don't even know it. It's cool cause we work under radar. All the glory goes to God. Put the righteousness God has given you to work.

CHOOSE

1st:

I'm set apart, it is required that I'm found faithful as a minister of Christ, an a steward of the mysteries of God. Behold, I'll show you a mystery. We shall not all sleep, but all will be changed. This has all been prearranged. Now life's in a greater view, I pursue everything that's in you. Dreams do come true, designing my flesh my best, I stay hard pressed. Evil heartless, but regardless, Christ the hardest, sins are confessed to The Lord and the darkness, can't comprehend nor can it bare it. It's God's will none should perish, it's my will all should hear it, share it, use it like a best, ware it.

CHOURS:

So whatcha whatcha whatcha want, I try to tell it too ya and ya still wanna front.

I say now whatcha, whatcha gonna be. A leader or a follower or somewhere in between.

I say now who now who now who you are, a drunk at the bar, a shooting star.

Tell me what now what now what it do, you better CHOOSE my dude or you gone loose.

2nd:

Just so you know I'm 00, lifting up Christ, splitting demons wigs to the white meat, in the home and the street. ŚqSound foreign don't it, never boring, the word of God on anointed beats. Firry darts repeal and bail back to hell where they dwelled from, 00 spiritual gun, I excel through righteousness not of me but of the Son, then the kick and the bass drum. Somebody listening to this song is gonna know today. Life and good, death and evil, pick and choose my people. I saw the dead small and great stand before God, poor to livin' large. Books were opened, all were in awe. Death and hell was cast into the Lake of Fire, this the second death, oh but you can save yourself.

CHORUS:

So whatcha whatcha whatcha want, I try to tell it too ya and ya still wanna front.

I say now whatcha, whatcha gonna be. A leader or a follower or somewhere in between.

I say now who now who now who you are, a drunk at the bar, a shooting star.

Tell me what now what now what it do, you better CHOOSE my dude or you gone loose.

3rd:

Choose this day who you will serve, I won't swerve when I server nerves with this word. You can come wit the force or the source, I'll shake the dust off my feet and continue north, we have a choice. I've seen the unseen from then to now, you can't hide from the Son of Man, that's out. Mix fruits produce troops, let His presence reign. No separation or division in the body man. When SOC was droppin' that Go Get It, I was praying to God that you would fear Him and hear them. All life as we know it will suddenly change. Things I'm saying won't sound so strange. Let ya know where I'm coming from I pray without ceasing meaning I pray till the Kingdom come, on accord with the body to the outcome, pray the Spirit pierce your heart threw your eardrum

(Chorus and Ending)

So whatcha whatcha whatcha want, I try to tell it too ya and ya still wanna front.

I say now whatcha, whatcha gonna be. A leader or a follower or somewhere in between.

I say now who now who now who you are, a drunk at the bar, a shooting star.

Tell me what now what now what it do, you better CHOOSE my dude or you gone loose.

SINGING

(I heard this from a friend who, heard this from a friend who, told me Jesus Christ wants to save your soul)

Joshua 24:14-16

14 "Now fear the Lord and serve him with all faithfulness. Throw away the gods your ancestors worshiped beyond the Euphrates River and in Egypt, and serve the Lord. 15 But if serving the Lord seems undesirable to you, then choose for yourselves this day whom you will serve, whether the gods your ancestors served beyond the Euphrates, or the gods of the Amorites, in whose land you are living. But as for me and my household, we will serve the Lord."
16 Then the people answered, "Far be it from us to forsake the Lord to serve other gods!

WHAT INSPIRED ME TO WRITE CHOOSE

I've stomped in Newark, Staten Island, Strong Island, Queens, Brooklyn, West Philly, DC, B-More, The GO, Detroit, Carolina N & S, Atlanta, Houston, Orlando, Tampa, South Beach Miami, Ocean Beach CA, Homestead, Liberty City, Daygo, so many more places I can't name them all. I've ran all these streets and more so would you think that they are calling me back. They are. All the time. But I'm a changed man. Yes it's a miracle I'm not dead when people drop dead from colds. My point is I'm changed, I'm a new man. 2 Corinthians 5:17 Therefore if any man [be] in Christ, [he is] a new creature: old things are passed away; behold, all things are become new. I'll say it one more time and meditate on every word you read. If any man [be] in Christ, [he is] a new creature: old things are passed away; behold, all things are become new.

    Joshua 24:15 And if it seem evil unto you to serve the Lord, choose you this day whom ye will serve; whether the gods which your fathers served that were on the other side of the flood, or the gods of the Amorites, in whose land ye dwell: but as for me and my house, we will serve the Lord..... All I'm sayin' is be real wit it. No more excuses, no more explanations. CHOOSE YOU THIS DAY. Me and my house, we have to make a decision. If not, we haven't made a choice and The Lord does not reign. I fight and die daily that The Lord reign in my house (my everything). Sorry if your not rolling wit me, but it means your against me and I ain't having it. Life will change drastically cause me and my house gonna do what we've been doing for years and not care what anybody thinks. Not gonna lose any sleep. People can say I'm hard, cold or whatever. Sorry but this time, can't hear ya. And if it seem evil unto you to serve the Lord, choose you this day whom ye will serve; whether the gods which your fathers served that were on the other side of the flood, or the gods of the Amorites, in whose land ye dwell, the gods of the flesh, the lust of the eyes, practicing disobedience, whatever; but as for me and my house, we will serve the Lord.

OPPORTUNITY

(Flowing rivers of living water, just let it be)

I'm Jeremiah Theres a fire burns inside of me, (just let lit be). Can't let it be, opportunity calling me so I hit the ground running like a comet coming through earths troposphere, stratosphere, mesosphere, thermosphere. Demons gonna fear 007 before the foundations of this world, born 11,11. It is what it has to be, (just let it be) my opportunity.

1st verse:

Let me take you pass the temporal to the eternal, I will return you, humm I'm guessing two minutes 45 seconds. Mama did her best an life's dramatic. Harry D never panic. 4 years old she left the planet. Catholic school was demanding, nuns commanding your complete attention, I never did listen. I'd rather be fishing, or in pop's liquor house listening to old cats. Starving for game you watch your own back. Cause around here only envy and greed preceded to lead the course of the day. There it is, I don't play. The American way, no matter what city or state, so much pain and hate got me prepared and armed for, sin demands an encore, but can't have it. Its victory in Jesus Christ so I snatched it

I'm Jeremiah theres a fire burns inside of me, just let it be. Can't let it be, opportunity calling me so I hit the ground running like a comet coming through earths troposphere, stratosphere, mesosphere, thermosphere demons gonna fear 007 before the foundations of this world, born 11,11. It is what it has to be, (just let it be) my opportunity.

2nd verse:

Since my life is like temporary momentarily I got your attention. Ordinarily would have battled and won by submission. Extra ordinary conditions put me in this position to petition the Lord Jesus Christ to intermission. So I intercede on your behalf. You ain't have to ask. Give you a blood bath that washes you white as snow. I put that on Cotton, Gegee, Sco, strait out Beatties Ford or off Skid Row. Christ coming to set stuff straight, thought you should know. Those that overcome shall be clothed in white raiment, this ain't a game kid. Christ set me up to be blameless, and I aim this flow to the masses. It don't take glasses to see what I'm sayin'. All creation complaining. Things will be done decent and in order, time getting shorter. Like a pot on a stove boiling over, can't compare to a super nova.

I'm Jeremiah theres a fire burns inside of me, just let it be. Can't let it be, opportunity calling me so I hit the ground running like a comet coming through earths troposphere, stratosphere, mesosphere, thermosphere demons gonna fear 007 before the foundations of this world, born 11,11. It is what it has to be, (just let it be) seized my opportunity.

Ephesians 5:16
making the most of every **opportunity**, because the days are evil.

Galatians 6:10
Therefore, as we have **opportunity**, let us do good to all people, especially to those who belong to the family of believers.

WHAT INSPIRED ME TO WRITE OPPORTUNITY

Opportunity. Opportunity is not given out all the time. But when you get an opportunity to change your world for the better, you better seize the moment. Opportunity is a bag of money sitting on 30th and El Cajon waiting for you to come pick up, it got your name on it. Opportunity not gonna hold your hand, get you a cab to come and get your money. On the other hand, if it's an opportunity you want, you will call to find what time the money will be there. You might stakeout 30th and El Cajon an scoop that cash before it can touch the hard concrete. That's the funny thing about opportunity, it don't care about your feelings or mine. If we miss it, the next in line is ready to cherish it and many die for it. My point is stay humble and check every opportunity. The one you slack on could be the one to bless you and your family for generations. We have embraced this opportunity to carry the cross. That's one of the reasons we Christ Walk. Jesus carried the cross to save the world. We follow His lead. If you had an opportunity to save the world, would you take it. That's what I thought. That's when a Christian would say send me Lord, send me.

THAT'S CHRISTMAS

1st verse

Good will peace on earth for what it's worth, it's gonna happen. God's gift bringing peace to mankind surpassing all understanding. Divine Son of God born of the Virgin Mary. We follow God's lead give gifts to our family and friends and folk with no ends. Make amends, reconcile this a time of love. Attributes of God through this baby I'm speaking of. Baby Jesus, born in a manger, the world changer, Emmanuel, God with us, no longer strangers. The wall torn down cause Jesus laid down His crown and came down to earth, took the form of a human birth. The start of His sacrifice for us. So much makes Him worthy to be praised. From baby to Great High Priest who intercedes. They have to see (your the biggest part of me)

CHORUS 2X

Put your hands up for baby Jesus, He's the reason for the season. All over the world we believers believe Him. The child's name is Jesus. Say it loud then, That's Christmas, This Christmas.

2nd VERSE

We need Christmas like we need fresh air. When it's all about giving, nothing to spare. You bring to the table if you're able, Jesus gave it all up, I gotsta call Him savior. This the season of His birth so we light up the city cause He's the light of the earth. That's what it's gonna take to change the hurt, the pain, the anger, the wicked. Most times it just slows down around Christmas. The atmosphere is shifting. People uplifting each other. But we gotta pray Christ is discovered not covered. The lover of my soul. I say it and it never gets old, oh how I praise the Ancient of Days, that you're ways become my ways. You gave so I gave and continue to give, that's Christmas. Its all about He not me, why (you're the biggest part of me)

CHORUS 2X

Put your hands up for baby Jesus, He's the reason for the season. All over the world we believers believe Him. The child's name is Jesus. Say it loud then, That's Christmas, This Christmas.

3rd VERSE

See I hit the streets my wife and me on Christmas Eve we see where there is a need. Just a few people that's hanging out doing nothing might be hungry. The Kingdom of Heaven is now apon'em. Bring'em home and feed'em a feast, eggs grits with cheese. Catfish, shrimp, sausage, bacon, seedless watermelon, everything there for the taking. Biscuits and gravy waiting. Praying for those that didn't have a prayer today. Give God the praise. Who else could orchestrate these ways. Love on strays, love on strangers. Love started by a baby in a manger. You may think it dangerous. But God be for me, who can be against me. This the season to give and I gots to give tremendously. Put in work like Allpeoples Church. Get Rocked, Get Real, Give it away. If Jesus stood here today I'd say (you're the biggest part of me)

CHORUS 3X

Put your hands up for baby Jesus, He's the reason for the season. All over the world we believers believe Him. The child's name is Jesus. Say it loud then, That's Christmas, This Christmas.

Luke 2:7-14

7 And she brought forth her firstborn son, and wrapped him in swaddling clothes, and laid him in a manger; because there was no room for them in the inn.
8 And there were in the same country shepherds abiding in the field, keeping watch over their flock by night.

9 And, lo, the angel of the Lord came upon them, and the glory of the Lord shone round about them: and they were sore afraid.
10 And the angel said unto them, Fear not: for, behold, I bring you good tidings of great joy, which shall be to all people.
11 For unto you is born this day in the city of David a Saviour, which is Christ the Lord.
12 And this shall be a sign unto you; Ye shall find the babe wrapped in swaddling clothes, lying in a manger.
13 And suddenly there was with the angel a multitude of the heavenly host praising God, and saying,
14 Glory to God in the highest, and on earth peace, good will toward men.

WHAT INSPIRED ME TO WRITE THAT'S CHRISTMAS

Just the real reason of Christmas. Even why we give gifts cause that's the main reason nowadays and it's not right. I mean kids don't pray before they eat, don't pray before they sleep. Jesus prayed often. If a person doesn't know that about Jesus, do you honestly think that they care on December 25 about Jesus. Why and how He was born. Where he was born and how it affected the world. Yes I tell you the real meaning in this song, the first Christmas song I've ever written.

    Of course when I wrote this I felt like people were sleeping on the song. Since I've been writing and making music I've felt like this. But no one never told me to stop. I had a show downtown once in the middle of the city and I remember just flowing. People wasn't dancing but just standing there listening and saying nothing. Then it occurred to me that they were listening to every word. It was the word of God that had everybody in awe. I know that's how it is on this song cause it's God's word. His only begotten son touching your life through your eardrums. I thank God for blessing me with this song as well as all the others. I love Christmas and wish it was everyday. It seems a time when we generally just care for our fellowman. Following Jesus's lead, who cared, was born and died for the world. That's Christmas.

STRETCH

I'm a say somethangs you never heard before. I speak power, you receive or ignore. Since I'm under radar haters can't see the score. I'm stealth mode, I seek and destroy. This the business I'm in, healing, seeking out sin. First within self, then within men. Ask me where I'm going, I'll tell you where I've been. I was born in sin, now I'm born again. The flow is blessed embrace the word of God. It's quick, powerful, sharper than any two edge sword. Piercing even to the dividing asunder of soul and spirit. Well it's about time one of y'all hear it. Is there anyone among you sick? Behold I bring health and healing, strength from illing, He sent His word and healed them. Abundance of peace and truth revealed to them, power went out from Him and healed them.

I'll restore health to you and heal you of your wounds. Homie they call you outcast and it ain't true. Come through, let us return to The Lord, yes He has torn but He will heal us in the name of Jesus. Make the call, the whole multitude out to touch Him, for power went out from Him and healed them all. My son's, give attention to my words, plant them in the midst of your heart and know that your set apart. They are life to all that find them, health to all their flesh. eternal game, given' you nothing less. I'll take sickness away from you bless your bread and water. Tables get turned up sickness get caught up. Heal me O Lord and I shall be healed, save me O Lord and I shall be saved, for you are my praise, show me your ways, stronger each day, I am what I am by Gods Grace

Is there anyone among you sick? Let him call for the elders of the church and let them pray over him or her. Anointing their head with oil in the name of The Lord. Prayer of faith will save the sick on accord, and The Lord will raise him up, and if he's committed sins he will be forgiven that's what's up. You need to practice what the real be. O Lord my God I cried out to you and you have healed me. Who forgives all your iniquities, who heals all your disease youth is renewed like the eagles wings. Seek His face be in health just as your soul prosper belove, for I'm The Lord who heals you, that's the covenant. Speak health and healing. I will heal them, by His stripes we are healed, teach the children. Speak health and healing, I will heal them, by His stripes we are healed, teach the children .

Luke 9:6
So they set out and went from village to village, proclaiming the good news and **healing** people everywhere.

Matthew 9:28-30
28 When he had gone indoors, the blind men came to him, and he asked them, "Do you believe that I am able to do this?"

"Yes, Lord," they replied.

29 Then he touched their eyes and said, "According to your faith let it be done to you"; **30** and their sight was restored. Jesus warned them sternly, "See that no one knows about this."

Luke 7:6-10
6 So Jesus went with them.
He was not far from the house when the centurion sent friends to say to him: "Lord, don't trouble yourself, for I do not deserve to have you come under my roof. **7** That is why I did not even consider myself worthy to come to you. But say the word, and my servant will be healed. **8** For I myself am a man under authority, with soldiers under me. I tell this one, 'Go,' and he goes;

and that one, 'Come,' and he comes. I say to my servant, 'Do this,' and he does it."
9 When Jesus heard this, he was amazed at him, and turning to the crowd following him, he said, "I tell you, I have not found such great faith even in Israel." **10** Then the men who had been sent returned to the house and found the servant well.

WHAT INSPIRED ME TO WRITE STRETCH

The way God set us up to receive healing. The way He speaks in His word and the directions He gives you to obtain healing for your body or even a situation. But first I gotta tell you a true story.

I was on the street in San Diego the other day talking to some mixed martial art fighters outside of their Gym on 30th and Ohio when somebody was calling my name. I turned around and it was the barber that cut my hair the other day. He was talking about getting his life back to the ways of God in short. I was telling him about the power of God and the miracles I've seen and some that God has worked through me. He said he had been looking allover for me. He had just pulled over to fix the car seat for his little girl when he saw me. He was telling me he needed help for that guy he was talking about the other day that had the problem with cigarettes. The guy was him. Cigarettes had him in the choke-hold.

    I was telling him if we lose ourselves in God, with that faith we can move mountains. Because we are God's people and He is our God, we should be constantly on the move tearing down strongholds in our lives and others. We are more than conquerors so we should always be moving forward. This is a movement and we are the movement so I prayed for him right there on the street and I got a feeling more than he got blessed that day. Confess your faults one to another, and pray one for another, that you may be healed. The effectual fervent prayer of a righteous man avail much. Let us keep practicing righteousness and move closer to God our father. In this you'll see healing like never before.

"I'M CRYIN' OUT RIGHT NOW"

Chorus:

I'm crying out, I'm crying out right now.

Not worthy of your sight, still you brought me back to life.

I'm crying out, I'm crying out right now. The gift of God through Christ, eternal life

1st Verse:

I thank God that He gave me a choice. I confess with my mouth, an I truly believe, God raised Jesus from the grave. After He died on the cross, listen to the sound of my voice. You were born to die, like my parents died, headed for the other side. But it wasn't time. No it wasn't time. I was snatched from the snare like a breath of fresh air. Hallelujah, higher and higher. The devil is a liar. Get behind me Satan, for it is written thou shalt worship the Lord thy God and Him only shalt thou serve.

Chorus:

I'm crying out, I'm crying out right now.

Not worthy of your sight, still you brought me back to life.

I'm crying out, I'm crying out right now. The gift of God through Christ, eternal life.

2nd verse:

You have a lot of trails and tribulations, you wonder why life's so hard. You wanna do the right thing, but no idea where to start. Cry out to Jesus, trust Him with all your heart. For by grace you've been saved through faith, not of yourself. It is the gift of God. Cause it's time, praise God it's time. He snatched me from the snare, like a breath of fresh air. Hallelujah, higher and higher. The devil is a liar. Get behind me Satan, for it is written thou shalt worship the Lord thy God and Him only shalt thou serve.

Chorus: I'm crying out, I'm crying out right now.

Not worthy of your sight, still you brought me back to life.

I'm crying out, I'm crying out right now. The gift of God through Christ, eternal life.

3rd :

We present this song to you, in order to share what we do. That you'd delight yourself in the Lord, and receive the desires of your heart. We would never force on you what we believe to be the absolute truth. The Lord is our rock, our fortress, our deliverer, our God. And if you agree and been set apart, for this time. Yes for this time. We're snatched from the snare, like breathes of fresh air. Hallelujah, higher and higher. The devil is a liar. Get behind us Satan, for it is written we shall worship the Lord thy God and Him only shall we serve.

Chorus:

I'm crying out, I'm crying out right now.

Not worthy of your sight, still you brought me back to life.

I'm crying out, I'm crying out right now. The gift of God through Christ, eternal life.

Deuteronomy 7:9
9 Know therefore that the Lord thy God, he is God, the faithful God, which keepeth covenant and mercy with them that love him and keep his commandments to a thousand generations;

1 Corinthians 2:9
9 But as it is written, Eye hath not seen, nor ear heard, neither have entered into the heart of man, the things which God hath prepared for them that love him.

Hebrews 11:6

6 But without faith it is impossible to please him: for he that cometh to God must believe that he is, and that he is a rewarder of them that diligently seek him.

WHAT INSPIRED ME TO WRITE I'M CRYIN' OUT RIGHT NOW

    Just the deepness God has placed in my heart. See I died in 2000. I might have told you that before but here's the deal, I'm still here. I still have my wife, Carol. I still have my family God has given me cause as a younger man I wasn't ready. He's been there all the time, every step of the way. Protected me from so many dangers seen an unseen. Can't even mention all the sin He has shielded me from that I would make it to this day. I know a few of y'all can relate to what I'm saying.

    My mother, Katherine Davis White who left the earth when I was 4. My father, Russell William White when I was 20. All these different emotions went into "Cryin' Out" because death has been a battle my whole life. It's always at the door and it's still at the door but because of God times are different. Death has no victory on me now. Can you kinda see why I wrote "Cryin' Out". It's because I'm constantly calling on God for everything. I gotta have Him in on everything. Even when I'm dead wrong, I'm crying out to God. He says in His word if I make my bed in hell, He is there. It's that attachment that got me to write this song.

So Job died, being old and full of days.=Job 42:17 / Ever heard the saying"It's better to burn out than fade away"? I disagree. You ever seen Micheal Jordan shoot a fade-away jump shot. Remember how deadly it was. You ever seen how deadly Kobe's fade-away from 3 point land is. It's like the shot is blocked, it's over and the man will not score then the fade comes into the equation. Bucket good and 1!! That's what I think about this Christ life and dying, being old and full of days. I'll keep talking about Jesus and the Kingdom of God until I'm dead. Yes I'd like to die of old age and lead someone to Christ on my dying bed. That would be so cool to save a life as I'm leaving this one. So I keep spreading the gospel until that day comes. Keep fighting the good fight. Keep praying and filling my days up with this Christ life. God bless you and keep Cryin' Out to God. This is never the END, only the BEGINNING.

DEDICATED TO CAROL E WHITE

Isaiah 40:31 But they that wait upon the Lord shall renew their strength; they shall mount up with wings as eagles; they shall run, and not be weary; and they shall walk, and not faint.

For two to become one is not an easy task. Harry and I met years before we married. I waited for him and he waited for me. Not willingly. He's an OG. Me, a woman with baggage, not willing to make another mistake. Many years in the making, we came together. Friendship grew as the wait went on. Then...Suddenly. Love was born.

"Everybody loves Harry." And, the words were true. Charisma and humility is what I saw. Arrogance was a word I heard. No. Confidence. Harry believes what God says about him. I have watched Harry Davis White do whatever the Lord puts before him. He doesn't hesitate to walk in faith. As I pondered our marriage, one of my many thoughts were Paul's words; "Follow me as I follow Christ". I saw a man who follows Christ.

Hopes and Dream fade into one.
My hopes, His dreams.
My dreams? His hopes?
Fade into One.
One Hope
One Dream
But... fading, not falling into One.
One.
No fade
No wear or tear.
If One
Not just one. two.
No, two become One.
ONE

Jesus is the capital One.

Poem by Carol White

Life Changer: we don't support each other. Never have, never will. At least on the level I'm talking about. If something drastic happens or a death, we come together. Don't even know why this is on my mind, it's not gonna change one heart. But I guess I got a hope in me and I'm built like this so I put true love out there. Not trying to preach but if I do, so what. What America needs now is love. The practice of it on every level. I've seen life, maybe the coldest person might run across this and it might change a situation. Save a life. Save some lives just cause they read this book. Makes sense now. An answer. I have to often keep myself encouraged cause my flesh tells me I'm wasting my time. Nobody gives a damn and they definitely not reading that goody goody crap I write. But then my Spirit. Oh, my Spirit. It has become so strong, especially when I'm weak like now, and says we will change the world. We will change lives. We will change generations. We will change atmospheres. We will change worlds. This is how my Spirit rolls. A change gone come, oh yes it is. A Life Changer..... 007

Regardless of what's going on in your life, I'm talking seen and unseen. God has made a way for you to obtain the fullest life if you want. You have a choice and Jesus died and rose from the grave that you have that choice. Still we disrespect Him, me included. But God is so deep He already knew we would do this so He made a contingency plan called repentance. If we tell Him we are sorry and ask Him to forgive us of our sins (disrespect cause God is Holy) He will do it if it's from the heart. The simple fact is most of us can't get by ourselves to see, hear, or receive the miracle right before our face. I call that seen and unseen peer pressure. God is real and you need to read His letter to you if you really want to know Him. Man can tell you anything, but God is not a man that He should lie.

Everything God has given me I've tried to use it to glorify Him. I've failed so many times. But as I become more seasoned, it looks to me that I glorify Him more and more everyday. Yes I was trying when I didn't know Him or His ways. I just knew He was top dog of all things. This was in me, nobody had to tell me this. So in all those years, through all the streets, cops, gangsters, enemies, setups, health issues, guns, drugs, and peer pressure, God set me here to present this: Life Changer.... 007

NOTES

NOTES

NOTES

NOTES

NOTES

Made in the USA
San Bernardino, CA
03 August 2017